D1361279

Mysterious Manatees

Florida A&M University, Tallahassee

Florida Atlantic University, Boca Raton

Florida Gulf Coast University, Ft. Myers

Florida International University, Miami

Florida State University, Tallahassee

University of Central Florida, Orlando

University of Florida, Gainesville

University of North Florida, Jacksonville

University of South Florida, Tampa

University of West Florida, Pensacola

University Press of Florida

Gainesville Tallahassee Tampa Boca Raton

Pensacola Orlando Miami Jacksonville Ft. Myers

In association with the Center for American Places

Santa Fe, New Mexico, and Harrisonburg, Virginia

Photographs and introduction by Karen Glaser

Text by John E. Reynolds III

mysterious Manatees

Published in cooperation with the Center for American Places.
This book was brought to publication with the generous assistance of an
anonymous patron of the Center for American Places. For more information about the center, visit its website (www.americanplaces.org).

08 07 06 05 04 03   6 5 4 3 2 1

Library of Congress Cataloging-in-Publication Data
Glaser, Karen.
Mysterious manatees / photographs and introduction by Karen Glaser;
text by John E. Reynolds III.
p. cm.
Includes bibliographical references.
ISBN 0-8130-2637-7 (cloth: alk. paper)
1. Manatees. 2. Manatees—Pictorial works. I. Reynolds, John Elliott, 1952-
II. Title.
QL737.S63G63 2003
599.55—DC21
2003040242

The University Press of Florida is the scholarly publishing agency
for the State University System of Florida, comprising Florida A&M
University, Florida Atlantic University, Florida Gulf Coast University,
Florida International University, Florida State University, University
of Central Florida, University of Florida, University of North Florida,
University of South Florida, and University of West Florida.

University Press of Florida
15 Northwest 15th Street
Gainesville, FL 32611-2079
http://www.upf.com

To the memory of my loving mother, Sylvia Glaser,

and my friend and neighbor, Martin Vanko.

—KG

To my many students, who make me very proud.

—JR

Contents

About This Book

Mysterious Manatees is the result of a unique partnership between an artist—photographer Karen Glaser—and a scientist—writer and scholar John E. Reynolds III. The book began in 1992 as a photographic project by Karen Glaser that led to a popular solo photographic exhibition of the work in 1996–97 at the Smithsonian Institution's National Museum of Natural History in Washington, D.C. The exhibit continued around the United States through 2002 as part of the Smithsonian Institution's Traveling Exhibition Service, and in 1997 another exhibit appeared at Centro Colombo Americano in Medellín, Colombia. Once the photographic sequence and introduction for the book were completed in 2001 under the aegis of the Center for American Places, John E. Reynolds III, a leading authority on the natural history of the manatee, came on board to write the accompanying text, completed under the aegis of the University Press of Florida. *Mysterious Manatees,* therefore, features the work—artistic and scientific—of two of the nation's leading interpreters of the life and underwater habitat of the manatee. It also represents a creative partnership between two institutions: the Center for American Places, a nonprofit organization, and the University Press of Florida, both of which are committed to bringing to publication books of lasting value on the natural and built environment.

George F. Thompson
President and Publisher
Center for American Places

Meredith Morris-Babb
Editor-in-Chief
University Press of Florida

Acknowledgments

I HAVE MANY PEOPLE to thank who helped make this book a reality. Tom Gilchrist, my friend and fellow diver, was the first person to describe manatees in detail to me so many years ago. A number of people at the Smithsonian helped the photographs reach a huge public audience. I met Amy Pasten of Smithsonian Publications at Fotofest in 1994. She liked the work very much and showed it to Marjory Stoller, who at the time was chief of Special Exhibitions at the National Museum of Natural History, Smithsonian Institution. Marjory's enthusiasm for my photographs and her persistence got the project rolling; she is the person who organized the *Mysterious Manatees* exhibition. I also thank Joe Madeira, current chief of Special Exhibitions for Natural History, who was Marjory's assistant at the time; his help was invaluable. I thank Daryl Domning and Jim Mead, who contributed the exhibition's text. Paula Kaufman, from the Office of Exhibits Central, carefully framed and readied the photographs for exhibition. I thank the folks at SITES who kept the exhibit traveling with ease from venue to venue: Cheryl Washer, Patsy-Ann Rasmussen, Michael Fox, and especially Jennifer Bine.

Bob Thall, my friend and colleague at Columbia College, Chicago, introduced me to his publisher, George F. Thompson, who served as the project director for this book. As current chairman of the Photography Department at Columbia College, Bob and his predecessor, John Mulvany, believed in my work and did what they could through the years to support the project, and I thank them for it. Bob also started me thinking about the new audience that a book would reach. About a year after our initial introduction, George Thompson and I met again through Martha A. Strawn at the publishing party for her amazing book *Alligators, Prehistoric Presence in the American Landscape,* which is part of the Center for American Places' Creating the North American Landscape series. We got to know one another in a much more casual setting during our task assigned by Martha: mixing traditional mint juleps for the crowd. George, president of the Center for American Places, is a man of integrity who works on projects he truly believes in, always offering support and insight. Randall B. Jones is George's right-hand man. What would we do without you, Randy? You're great.

Throughout this project, I have had outstanding help and support from talented, energetic student interns and assistants. These people are the nuts and bolts of this project, and I couldn't have done it without them. They are Amee Turner, Diana Vallera, Jackie Ansted, Barbara Rodgers, Victor Leon, Claire Mooney, Alexis Wolf, Suzy Poling, and John Paul Doguin.

When shooting for this project, I called the Best Western Crystal River Resort my home. The manager, Frances Roberts, has become my friend and was the one who made that place so comfortable for us. She always tried to get us our favorite room and would on occasion go diving with us—not to mention her talent for making out-of-this-world key lime pie. The Crystal Lodge Dive Center at the Best Western is my base of operation. Jerry Hogan is the owner and Darren Wilkes is the manager. To Jerry, Darren, and all of their guys, past and present, you are always accommodating, helpful, colorful, and funny. To Evon Streetman, an amazing photographer from Florida, you are a mentor. You know how to live right! My husband, John, and I thank you for your hospitality on all of our Florida trips. Your friendship means a lot.

Manatee experts are friendly people. Bob Bonde, from the Sirenia Project in Gainesville, has been helpful through the years in answering my many manatee questions. While I was writing my introduction, Bob referred me to Tom O'Shea to answer a specific question about manatee sounds and vocalizations, as this area is more Tom's expertise. I've never met Tom, but the information he provided helped a great deal. Ruby Montoya helped me early on in this project in learning about manatees in Colombia. I also wish to thank the late Jesse White for his efforts in helping to educate the public about this mammal.

My trip to Colombia was a special experience. Juan Alberto Gaviria, gallery director at Centro Colombo Americano and now my friend, made it all possible. I also thank the director of the center, Paul Bardwell, for his hospitality and help. Ricardo Botero, Rafael Vidal, and Gustavo Gonzalez—you all love manatees and I want to thank you for your efforts in public education and awareness.

To Meredith Morris-Babb at the University Press of Florida, thanks for believing in this book and for bringing John Reynolds on board. John, you are so knowledgeable about manatees and your text is not only very informative and interesting, but also heartfelt and personal. Thanks for being a partner in this great project.

Jocelyn Nevel has been a good friend who has allowed me to bounce edits, ideas, and revisions off of her throughout the project. Joan Morgenstern, you are a kind woman with a clear and special passion for photographs. Your involvement and contribution to this medium means a lot. Thank you.

My late mother, Sylvia Glaser, was always there showing love and support. My father, Robert Glaser, taught me through example how important it is to spend your life doing what you love.

Last, but certainly not least, is my husband, John Stranick, my constant companion throughout this project. John has been everything from boat captain to assistant, from picture editor to chief cook and bottle washer. He loves the adventure as much as I do. We are an excellent team and have a lot of fun!

Karen Glaser

I am grateful to a number of people who provided insights or information used in this book. Among them are Sara Shapiro (biologist) and Colonel Don Holway and Leslie Woodard (law enforcement) with the State of Florida; Don McKinney, a guide in southwestern Florida; Kiefer Gier, with the National Park Service; Dr. Douglas Nowacek (acoustician) from Mote Marine Laboratory; Dr. Tom Oberhofer (economist) with Eckerd College; Dr. Buddy Powell (biologist) from Wildlife Trust; and Rolland Freeman (my pilot).

I also thank people who read drafts of parts or all of the manuscript for this book and provided valuable comments: Jason Allen, Dr. Dave Duncan, Dr.

Richard Flamm, Dr. Elsa Haubold, Teresa Kessenich, Dr. Catherine Langtimm, Dr. Doug Nowacek, Dr. James Powell, Meghan Pitchford, Dr. Tim Ragen, Patrick Rose, James Valade, and Dr. Dana Wetzel. The book manuscript was reviewed by two experts on sirenian biology and management, Drs. Daryl Domning and Dan Odell, both of whom offered excellent insights and suggestions. I appreciated everyone's input, but note that persistent flaws in the text are mine.

My thanks also go to longtime friend and marine science colleague Gregg Brooks, with whom I discussed aspects of the book and who accompanied me on my trip to Everglades City. I would have preferred for him to buy me lunch there. And a beer.

Meredith Morris-Babb at University Press of Florida was, as usual, delightful to work with and forgiving of my occasional delays. Kate McKean of UPF and Amanda Chunco of Mote Marine Laboratory were extremely helpful as I prepared the manuscript. And Karen Glaser, whom I met during her whirlwind trip to Florida in December 2001, deserves, perhaps, the most thanks, for sharing her talents and photographs with us all.

John E. Reynolds III

part I   science

Those Were the Days . . .

IN THE LATE 1940s, lots of things were different in southwestern Florida from what they are today. Rolland (Bud) Freeman was just a teenager at that time, and he spent his summers working out of Everglades City. As a native of southwestern Florida (specifically Sarasota), Bud's eyes have witnessed a lot of changes in that part of the world, and today he sometimes recalls how he and other folks spent their time and supported themselves back then. Bud reminisces about accompanying Dr. Frank McKinley and Deaconess Harriett Bedell of the Glade Cross Mission on their rounds, as they ministered to the local Mikosukkee Indians as well as to the white and black residents; he remembers traveling quiet waterways in the Ten Thousand Islands, savoring the stillness, the wildlife, and the enjoyment of fishing or hunting for the pot; his eyes light up as he recounts stories of the time when he worked on a run boat for the Riggs Fish Company, for whom he helped to transport huge catches of freshly caught mullet from the Shark and Harney Rivers north to the big city—Everglades City; and he shakes his head in some disbelief as he thinks about the days before air conditioning and mosquito repellents. Get Bud started and the details he recalls are pretty amazing. However, I find one of the details he *doesn't* recall just as fascinating as what he does: Bud doesn't remember seeing or hearing much about manatees while he was in Everglades City in the 1940s.

I wondered why manatees, often called *sea cows* by folks in Florida, are such common topics of conversation (and argument!) today, but were not much a part of Bud's memories. To attempt to unravel the question, I visited Bud's old haunts in December 2001. I had not been to Everglades City for many years. I entered the town a little after noon. Never one to miss a meal, I responded to my appetite by stopping for something to eat at the Rod and Gun Club, looking much as it did in the 1920s, when Barron Collier bought it as a private club where he hosted prominent guests, including several U.S. presidents, interested in spectacular hunting and fishing. After lunch, I wandered through the bustling town of 479 residents.

It seemed that December day as if time has stood still in lots of ways in Everglades City. The town still seems hewn out of the surrounding mangrove swamps—a place where humans exist, but do not yet dominate the landscape as they do in much of Florida. In one of Peter Matthiessen's wonderful, brooding books, *Lost Man's River,* one of the key characters was blind, but was often able to use his other senses to tell where he was in the natural maze provided by the Ten Thousand Islands, where Everglades City lies. Although I certainly lack that sort of ability, I stood outside the Rod and Gun Club, closed my eyes, and let my other senses absorb stimuli I had missed for awhile: the tangy, sulfurous smell emanating from the dense, luxuriant stands of red, black, and white mangroves; the soft texture of the southerly breeze, a welcome relief a couple of days after passage of a mild early cold front, as it wrapped essences of tropical Caribbean islands around me; the hum of insects, entering my consciousness at first, but subtly fading to white noise; and the intensity of the sun, even in winter. Even without opening my eyes, I knew roughly where I was right away—and it did not feel like part of one of the fastest growing states in the United States. It felt like a good place for manatees and other critters.

I ultimately found my way down to the Gulf Coast Ranger Station for the Everglades National Park, past the little airstrip where avid sport fishermen arrive from around the state. The station, located south of the town off the two-lane road to Chokoloskee, is a good jumping-off spot for people who want to learn a little about and to "experience" the Everglades and its wildlife. I was curious to discover whether people who spend a lot of time on the water in 2001 (as Bud had 50 or so years earlier) consider manatees a rarity. I approached Kiefer Gier, one of the park rangers, who is a relative newcomer to southwestern Florida's coast and who takes a particular interest in manatees. I got the response from Kiefer that I predicted: far from being a rarity, seeing 20–25 manatees near the seagrass beds west of the station is almost an everyday event, except during the coldest days of winter, when they swim to the Faka Union Canal where the water is a bit warmer, or even up to the power plant discharge on the Orange River in Fort Myers.

I also was fortunate enough to track down well-known fishing guide Don McKinney. Don has been a guide down around Chokoloskee for the past 35 years—I guess that means he has probably spent nearly 100,000 hours on the waters of that region. Don ventured that manatees have always been present in the area during his lifetime. Back in the old days, he noted that manatees occasionally got hit and killed by boats and that when a fresh manatee carcass appeared, local folks butchered it and ate well. As expected, Don confirmed the greater abundance of manatees in recent years—"schools of six or eight" are not uncommon today. They're apparently not yet as thick as the mosquitoes, but . . .

So . . . at least from the manatees' perspective around Everglades City, these just might be the days!

One might wonder how the status of manatees could apparently be better in the fast-paced early days of the twenty-first century than in the "good old days." At a time when we hear so much about human exploitation of the natural world (among other things), how could a slow-breeding, slow-moving coastal marine mammal do better now than in the good old days of the past? I guess the answer depends on for whom the good old days were actually good, or how long ago the good old days actually were.

Sirenians (the group of animals to which modern manatees belong) have occupied waters of what are now the Caribbean Sea and the United States for tens of millions of years. The earliest time that scientists have documented the existence of *Trichechus manatus* (the species to which Florida manatees belong) is from the early Pleistocene epoch, about 1.5–1.1 million years ago. Incongruously, one still encounters people and papers that mistakenly suggest that manatees are not native to Florida and that elimination of presumed exotic species such as the manatee makes some sense for the good of the state's coastal and riverine environments. The real newcomer to the state (1.49–1.09 million years after *Trichechus manatus* arrived, if anyone is counting) is the species *Homo sapiens.* Ironically, this is the same species that has been the primary threat to manatees and many other species around the globe. On reflection, perhaps removal of the newer species from Florida isn't such a hot idea after all!

There is evidence that manatees have been hunted in Florida (and elsewhere throughout their range) for perhaps 10,000 years, since the Paleo-Indian period when Florida was first occupied by aboriginal Indians. Although it is uncertain exactly how the primitive Paleo-Indians were able to kill such large aquatic animals, the presence of manatee bones in archeological sites suggests that manatees were consumed on occasion. The extent to which manatee hunting occurred and the number of manatees that existed in Florida historically remain shrouded by the years and by a deficiency in historical accounts.[1]

By the time Europeans arrived in Florida around 1500, there were possibly around 25,000 aboriginal Indians living at a subsistence level in the state. That tiny number, scattered throughout the state, is in the same ballpark as the number of visitors to Disney's Magic Kingdom and to SeaWorld in Orlando on a single busy day; alternatively, 25,000 people represent about one-third to one-quarter of the people present at a Tampa Bay Buccaneers football game on a given Sunday. The relatively small number of inhabitants present 500 years ago didn't persist very well; within 200 years, most of the descendants of the original human occupants of Florida were eliminated by introduced diseases and other factors. With the eradication of competition, Indians from the north, collectively called Seminoles, moved into the state, along with more and more white settlers. The Seminoles actively hunted manatees for their meat, hides, and oil, and they traded unused meat and other products to the settlers. Among the better historical descriptions of a Seminole hunt for manatees is one by Charles B. Cory, from 1896:

Many of these animals are killed by the Indians every year. They hunt them in canoes, sometimes in the river, and again in the ocean, but usually near the mouth of some river. These animals come to the surface every few minutes to breathe and their heads may be seen as they appear for a moment above the surface of the water.

They harpoon them as they rise to the surface using a steel point barbed on one side, attached to the end of a long pole. To the steel point is fastened a strong cord, which in turn is attached to a float. Upon being struck the manatee sinks at once, but the direction in which he moves is indicated by the float. The Indians follow the float as closely as possible and watch for him to rise to the surface, when they shoot him through the head, and the huge animal is towed to shore. It requires considerable skill as well as strength to drive the harpoon through the thick, tough hide. Many of those animals grow to be very large size, and it is claimed that some of them have been taken which exceed twelve feet in length.[2]

The white settlers did not simply trade with Indians for manatee meat and other products—they were active hunters as well. Colorful accounts such as those in Oppel and Meisel's *Tales of Old Florida* provide some interesting glimpses into manatees and manatee hunters. The animals were sometimes shot, but more often they were harpooned. Manatees may have a reputation among modern schoolchildren and other enthusiasts as "gentle giants," but they are actually pretty tough customers. One animal that recently died and was examined by scientists to determine its cause of death had scar patterns that indicated he had been struck 50 separate times by motorboats during his life. A bullet or two back in the old days simply may not have killed a manatee right away, meaning that the hunter might well lose his quarry. To prevent or reduce the risk of such losses, hunters used methods similar both to those described above for Seminole hunters and to those still employed today by native hunters of manatees and their cousin the dugong around the world. In such cases, an animal was harpooned, but a line with a float was attached to the harpoon so that the hunter could follow the wounded manatee. When the manatee tired, it could be approached and hit on the head or repeatedly lanced or shot until it died.

As is the case for hunting by Indians, the magnitude of take of manatees by the white settlers remains unknown. It is well established, however, that settlers enjoyed eating manatee meat, especially the tail, soaked in brine. In fact, records and oral tradition maintain that manatee meat is excellent to eat and that it comes in several flavors, ranging from strong, like beef, to mild, like veal. This seemingly fanciful idea is actually easy to believe, given the various hues and textures of the muscle from different parts of the body of a manatee. Other useful products besides meat were also derived from manatee hunting; they included the fat, used for cooking and medicinal purposes, the extremely dense bones, which were sometimes carved into beautiful ivory-like artifacts, and the tough, thick hides, from which walking sticks, oarlocks, whips, and many other products were crafted. At least some of the products wound up in markets in Havana, as Cuban fishermen exploited the largesse of Florida's coastal waterways.

By 1893, manatees were noticeably scarce in Florida, and the state passed its first legislation to prohibit killing of the disappearing mammals. One writer, worried about the fate of manatees in 1880, wrote:

But before many years shall pass away the scene will change. Civilization is encroaching: the restless settler is every year pushing farther and farther into the unknown wilds of Florida, and even now men are casting ahead to secure a homestead or to commence a speculation in some way in the lands or products of this region. Then it will surely happen that the peace-loving manatee will be driven away and they will become a legend or old man's tale.[3]

Oddly (or luckily) enough, manatees do not appear to have been the primary target for the hardy early explorers of the Sunshine State, although trade in manatee products did exist. Back in those days, humans actively exploited nearly every living resource in sight in the state, naïvely assuming (if they even thought about it at all) that the abundance of Florida's wildlife could not possibly be diminished. Rather, these men (and even a few women) sought both widely marketable commodities such as gator hides and exotic plumes from a variety of birds, and the thrill of bagging a huge tarpon or shark. The effects on some species are still not negligible today. Manatees appear to have represented more a rare, prized dinner than a regular source of revenue.

Another type of manatee hunting evolved in the early 1900s. The development of the New York Aquarium and other such facilities created a market for living manatees. In his delightful book *Florida Enchantments,* written in 1908, A. W. Dimock described the methodical capture of manatees for exhibit as curiosities. To attempt to minimize harm to the animals, hunters such as Dimock chased them in boats until they were tired and then entangled them in seine or cast nets. Naturally, some of the manatees captured in this manner died . . . but another ready market, associated with science museums, existed for cleaned skeletons and hides, which brought up to about $100 per manatee.

Yes, 100 years or so ago, manatees in Florida were captured and killed with regularity for the pot, for their leather and other products, for some extra cash, and for the amazement and amusement of the public. It appears that the "good old days" were quite a rough time to be a manatee in Florida! Nonetheless, the manatees there were luckier than their cousins to the south.

As far as anyone knows, the only place where manatees have ever been hunted as a major commercial venture was in Brazil in the 1930s–50s. Renowned manatee biologist/paleontologist Daryl Domning documented that many tens of thousands of manatee skins were exported (for use as an extremely tough leather) between 1935 and 1954. In the late 1950s, the primary product of manatee hunts was the meat, which was salted, packed, exported, and sold as a product called *mixira.*

The primary species of manatee taken in these hunts was the Amazonian manatee (*Trichechus inunguis*), a relative of the species native to Florida, which is called the West Indian manatee (*Trichechus manatus*). In fact, the manatee that lives in Florida is morphologically distinguishable as a separate subspecies of the West Indian manatee, appropriately named the Florida manatee (*Trichechus manatus latirostris*).

To this point, I have mentioned that hunting for a variety of reasons historically created undocumented levels of impacts on the number of manatees in Florida. So did Nature.

Manatees in Florida occupy the northern fringe of the range of the West Indian manatee. This means that manatees in Florida are exposed periodically to cold temperatures, a stress that the species is poorly adapted to survive. To begin with, manatees have an extremely low metabolic rate, about 15–20 percent of the rate that one would expect for animals their size. Add to this rate the fact that water transfers heat away from a body 25 times faster than is the case in air, and the Florida manatee is a prime candidate for death, or at least severe stress, from hypothermia during winter. As long ago as 1895, Outram Bangs noted that dead manatees appeared during and after the onset of very cold weather in Florida, and as many as 46 cold-related deaths of manatees have been reported recently during a single frigid winter (1989–90).

Thus cold weather has impaired manatee survival in both historical and modern times. Possibly the mortality was higher in the past (although we don't know this), because artificial sources of warm water, as at power plants, were not present and exploitable by manatees until the middle of the twentieth century.

Nature dealt manatee numbers additional blows at times. In April 1996, nearly 150 manatees died from the effects of a red tide outbreak in southwestern Florida; other, lesser outbreaks have led to smaller die-offs of manatees as well in recent years. Red tides are produced by small marine organisms called *dinoflagellates,* which produce a toxin called *brevetoxin.* Inhalation or ingestion of brevetoxin can cause illness or even death in fish, birds, and mammals, including manatees and humans. Since red tide blooms have existed at least for many centuries, one can only assume that manatees occasionally succumbed to this natural toxin in the past.

Differences over time in the impacts of natural events such as cold weather and red tide blooms are hard to assess retrospectively, and not simply because we may lack written records documenting such events. There are suggestions that agricultural runoff in rivers leading into the Gulf of Mexico may exacerbate the frequency and intensity of red tides along the west coast of Florida today. Certainly manatee distribution in winter in Florida has changed, as artificial warm-water discharges provide havens (or traps, depending on one's perspective) that never existed for the animals prior to the middle of the twentieth century. One thing is certain: human impacts on environments and on species have changed considerably over time.

Humans can sometimes be a little romantic (even myopic!) when they discuss "the good old days" when life was simpler and in many ways thought of or recalled as better. Without the benefit of rose-colored glasses, the world may not look quite the same, especially for the nonhuman residents. In what some might call the "good old days" before my friend Bud Freeman lived in Everglades City, manatees seem to have been hunted for a lot of reasons. Even into the 1970s and 1980s, butchered manatees were reported, and not just in places that are remote from civilization. In 1980, two butchered carcasses showed up in the Miami River; in 1985, a fisherman along the populous east coast of the state was convicted of killing a manatee for meat. One cannot help wondering: Do manatees really have any "good old days"?

Bud Freeman now works as my pilot when we do aerial surveys of Sarasota County waters, and it is a poor survey day if we see fewer than 50 manatees, except during cold weather when the animals seek refuge in naturally and artificially produced warm-water discharges outside of the Sarasota Bay area. The same phenomenon occurs when scientists take to the air to search for and count manatees in many other coastal parts of the state as well. Like the guides and rangers around Everglades City, fishermen, boaters, naturalists, and others who frequent Florida's waterways comment on the apparent surfeit of manatees.

Science supports the idea that manatees exist in greater numbers now than they did in Bud's youth or during much of the time since then. Using long-term photographic catalogs of distinctly scarred manatees, scientists have calculated survival estimates for adult manatees in several parts of the state. Such estimates suggest that, for the four subpopulations of manatees that exist in Florida, the two smaller ones (in northwestern Florida and in the upper St. Johns River) have increased since the 1970s and continue to increase; the large subpopulation occupying the east coast of Florida appears to have increased into the early to mid-1990s, after which time it seems to have stabilized or even started to decrease. The verdict is still out regarding the status of the large subpopulation along the central western and southwestern coast of Florida, although exceptionally high levels of both human-related and natural mortality of manatees there make some scientists believe that this group, like its Atlantic coast cohort, may be slipping a bit.[4]

The trends suggested by the adult survival estimates are reinforced by analyses of some long-term aerial survey data, providing independent reinforcement that the trends are real. What both scientific approaches suggest is that the "good old days" for manatees in Florida occurred only about a decade ago. Following many decades—even centuries—of hunting pressure, I believe that manatee populations around the state were permitted to rebound through the 1970s, 1980s, and early 1990s—a relative golden age for Florida's manatees! However, a new threat, or more accurately a suite of threats, has started to replace hunting, with the recent result that the two largest subpopulations of manatees appear to be stable at best. The recent threats to the long-term prospects for manatees have to do with a variety of factors, mostly related to the unprecedented and poorly managed growth of the human population in Florida.

As an immigrant to Florida from the Middle Atlantic states almost 30 years ago, I was awestruck by the open spaces and the richness of the natural resources in my new home state. A lot of people have moved to Florida for just that reason—and who can blame them? But the population growth of the state threatens the quality and quantity of the very resources that draw many people to the state in the first place. I noted that the native population at the time that Europeans discovered Florida was about 25,000; by 1950 (when my friend Bud prowled the waterways of Everglades City), the human population had increased more than two orders of magnitude, to about 2.7 million. In the 50 years since then, the population increased by a factor of seven, to around 16 million, and in the next 30 years, experts predict that the number of people will double to nearly 32 million residents. At that point, the human population will have increased more than a thousandfold from what it was prior to European settlement.

The effects on habitat have already been huge. Through the mid-1970s, an average of approximately 29,000 hectares (71,630 acres) of Florida's wetland was lost annually; this is an alarmingly large number, especially if one considers that, prior to development of the state, there existed 500,000 hectares (1,235,000 acres) of wetland. This means that the annual loss documented 30-odd years ago approximated almost 6 percent of the original extent of wetlands. Much of the wetland loss involved conversion to farmland, which one could argue can be somewhat less damaging to the environment and to wildlife than is conversion to towns or cities. However, the current rate of conversion of farmland and other rural areas to urban ones is 52,630 hectares (130,000 acres) each year. Recall that such figures, staggering as they may be, apply during a time considerably before the human population reaches its zenith (or nadir, depending on one's point of view). One has to wonder how people, with all their ingenuity, will manage to balance the gargantuan needs of an expanding human population with an ability to maintain even modest natural resources and environmental quality.

The antediluvian manatee may have seen its heyday not so long ago—just a decade. If that is the case, then focused, productive, informed, and collective efforts may still recapture the conditions needed to maintain those times, without undue restriction to Florida's human residents and their still-arriving immigrant kin. Ultimately—even soon—we need some better balance if we hope to maintain quality of life for human and nonhuman residents of Florida in the decades to come. The keys involve recognizing the challenges and taking proactive steps to address them. But right from the start, there is one truth that must be recognized and addressed: there are finite limits to what manatees can do to adjust to more people and to more impacts from people. The burden of adjustment, if there truly is a will to maintain Florida's wild species such as manatees, must fall on the species with greater adaptability, ingenuity, and capacity to create and destroy, namely the humans.

This book discusses some of the challenges to achieving that balance, and it offers some suggestions. It attempts to paint neither bad guys nor good guys. It simply provides some facts and figures about manatees and deals with the issue of trying to let manatees and people coexist in an increasingly crowded world. It recognizes that our approaches to balance have generally failed miserably all over the world—even in places where humans are relatively sparse. It asks that we consider new paradigms and new partnerships for the mutual good of ourselves and the species whose survival depends on our willingness to share. The evocative photographs in this book suggest, as do Clyde Butcher's haunting Everglades landscapes, a simple and somehow mysterious world that can be attained and maintained if we look hard enough and value it intensely enough.

All in the Family

Sirens Past and Present

chapter 2

ANIMALS, PLANTS, AND OTHER ORGANISMS are classified and grouped based on their relative similarities and differences. The study of relationships among organisms is called *systematics,* and the classification scheme systematists (scientists who do systematics) use today has been around nearly 300 years, since it was honed and popularized by a Swedish naturalist, Carolus Linnaeus, in the eighteenth century. And the system works well and makes intuitive sense much of the time: it is easy, after all, for people to guess that tigers and lions are closely related or that dolphins and porpoises are "cousins."

Manatees, with their mélange of characteristics, created a conundrum for early naturalists in terms of their affinities and relationships with other mammals. Around the start of the nineteenth century, the verdict was in: manatees were simply unusual tropical and subtropical walruses.

A glance at the faces of a manatee and a walrus shows some striking similarities: small eyes, large upper lips with vibrissae (whiskers), small valve-like nostrils, and a generally bulbous appearance. In fact, a close relative of the manatees (called the dugong) actually has walrus-like tusks. Who could blame the naturalists who claimed that manatees and walruses were closely related?

Systematists actually use an arsenal of tools and techniques to assess relatedness among organisms. Whereas facial appearance is not irrelevant, other factors can weigh even more heavily. For example, a whole range of anatomical characteristics may be used for comparisons of species for which people suspect relatedness. And, in fact, appearances in animals, as in people, can be deceiving.

The process of natural selection shapes the adaptations and features that organisms display. Thus, similarity of anatomical features could reflect one of a couple of possibilities. The first is that organisms that appear similar could have a close common ancestry; after all, brothers and sisters may have similar features that they inherited from their parents—what we call a family resemblance. On the other hand, organisms that appear similar could have no close common ancestry whatsoever and could, instead, have been shaped through natural selection by exposure to the same sorts of environmental features; when this shaping occurs, scientists call it *evolutionary convergence*. A good example of a convergent feature is the wing of a butterfly compared with that of a bird.

Manatees and their relatives are members of an order of mammals called the Sirenia, a fanciful name that reflected sailors' and others' beliefs that these animals were the Sirens of Greek mythology. Today people who romantically still associate manatees with the mythical Sirens tend to call them mermaids.

The sirenians represent one of the three living orders of mammals that include marine representatives. The other marine mammals are included in the order Carnivora (meat eaters such as walruses, seals, sea lions, sea and marine otters, and the polar bear) and the order Cetacea (the whales, dolphins, and porpoises). Members of the general public tend to lump all the marine mammals together—symbolically, ecologically, legislatively, and systematically. There is some merit in all of these perspectives, except the systematic one.

In reality, the fact that some species of seals, sirenians, and whales share common anatomical and other features reflects evolutionary convergence that occurred simply because the adaptations that led to the success of these groups were "selected" by what worked best for those mammals living in the water. Thus, the various cetaceans, marine carnivores, and sirenians tend to be large and well insulated (for heat retention), streamlined (to facilitate moving through the water), good divers (relative to humans and other terrestrial mammals), and possessed of a fluke or paddle-like appendages for locomotion. However, despite the number and variety of their similarities, in reality the three orders of marine mammals, we now know, arose from dramatically different ancestral lineages (see table 1).

Not too surprisingly, the carnivorous marine mammals arose from terrestrial carnivores. There is some controversy surrounding the origins of the

Table 1. The relationships of the sirenians and other marine mammals.[a]

Kingdom Animalia (includes all animals)

Phylum Chordata (includes a wide range of animals that are unified by traits such as the presence of pharyngeal gill slits at some point in their lives, a dorsal hollow nerve cord [called a spinal cord], and a rod of supportive tissue called a *notocord* [in humans called a spine]; excludes all invertebrates)

    Subphylum Vertebrata (includes fishes, amphibians, reptiles, birds, and mammals, all of which possess a true backbone)

    Class Mammalia (includes species with features such as mammary glands, hair, a muscular diaphragm, and, with a couple of exceptions, *viviparity* [birth to "live young" as opposed to laying eggs])

        Order Sirenia (includes manatees and dugongs)
            Family Trichechidae: manatees
            Family Dugongidae: dugong

        Order Cetacea (includes whales, dolphins, and porpoises)
            Thirteen families of cetaceans

        Order Carnivora (includes meat-eating mammals)
            Family Ursidae: polar bear
            Family Mustelidae: sea otter and marine otter
          Suborder Pinnipedia: flipper-footed mammals
            Family Otariidae: sea lions and fur seals
            Family Phocidae: "true" seals
            Family Odobenidae: walrus

[a]The general scheme outlined above is consistent with that developed almost 300 years ago by Linnaeus and is based on relative similarities and differences among organisms.

cetaceans, but compelling evidence suggests that the whales, dolphins, and porpoises arose from terrestrial hoofed ancestors, specifically from, or close to, the even-toed ungulates called *artiodactyls*. Notwithstanding the complicated name, artiodactyls include some everyday mammals such as cows, pigs, and sheep, as well as more exotic animals such as camels and hippopotamids.

The sirenians arose from a dramatically different group, collectively called the *subungulates,* or *Paenungulata*. The three other orders with extant (living) members often included in the subungulate group are the Proboscidea (elephants), Hyracoidea (small, furry animals called hyraxes or conies), and Tubulidentata (aardvarks). Also closely related to the sirenians (and even more closely related to the proboscideans), but extinct for several million years, was a group of hippopotamus-like animals called *desmostylians*. How, one might legitimately wonder, did harebrained scientists decide to lump together such a diverse (and strange!) group of animals?

The answer lies near the start of this chapter: systematists use an array of tools, and appearances may be deceiving. One of the most powerful sets of tools available to scientists today involves examinations of similarities at the molecular level. For example, it is possible—even pretty easy—today to assess aspects of the genetic makeup for species, and genes, after all, provide direct evidence of heredity. It is also routine to examine proteins, which are made up of strings of amino acids, the sequence of which is tightly choreographed by the sequence of bases (called *nucleotides*) that make up genes. Thus, similarities in protein structure or components provide strong evidence for genetic similarities, and hence for common ancestry.

Analysis of certain proteins (for example, α-crystallinA) provides strong support for the ties among the subungulates, as well as for the fact that the various subungulate orders are more similar to one another than they are to anything else. In addition, there are bits of other evidence to support the relationship: similarities in certain dental features, absence of a clavicle (collarbone), the presence of nails or hooves rather than of claws, and a herbivorous diet (except for the ant-and-termite-eating aardvarks).

The sirenians split from their terrestrial subungulate ancestors about 50 to 55 million years ago, during the Eocene epoch. Although the oldest sirenian fossils are from Jamaica, paleontologists believe that the group originated in the Old World, in Eurasia and/or in Africa. The profound adaptations to an aquatic lifestyle that sirenians acquired took a long time, but within 5–10 million years of their appearance, several genera of sirenians existed, and within 20 million years of their appearance the sirenians had become extremely well adapted to their new watery environment and had diversified even more. During the Oligocene and Miocene epochs (35 million to 5 million years ago), the fully aquatic sirenians reached their peak in diversity and spread into new regions of the world. In the Miocene epoch (25 million to 5 million years ago), in particular, tropical conditions favorable to survival and diversification of sirenians were widespread.

Today there are only four extant species: three manatees and one dugong. The earliest sirenian that was truly manatee-like in appearance was called *Potamosiren*. It appeared about 15 million years ago, during the Miocene epoch (the oldest fossils are from Colombia). The manatees and manatee-like sirenians (collectively called *trichechids*) diversified and became more similar to modern manatees later in the Miocene.

The dugong-like sirenians (called *dugongids*) are much more diverse in the fossil record than are the trichechids, even though there remains only a single species of dugong today. The dugongids also diversified and became widely distributed much earlier than the trichechids, during the Eocene epoch. Fossil remains of dugongids have been reported from deposits in countries bordering the Mediterranean Sea, western Europe, the Caribbean Sea, the southeastern United States, South America, the North Pacific Ocean, and the Indian Ocean. The most widespread genus of dugongid was *Metaxytherium,* which lived during the Miocene epoch and which appears to have given rise to a new subfamily of dugongids that included Steller's sea cow, an unusual sirenian that occupied cold, temperate waters of the North Pacific and was hunted to extinction about 250 years ago.

As is true of other species as well, the manatees and other sirenians evolved in ways that were constrained by the local environment occupied by the animals. Factors such as food availability, temperature, predators, and competition all determine the species that succeed or that perish in particular ecosystems. The greater diversity of sirenians in past times indicates that, for whatever reasons, these animals were able to adapt in ways that allowed them to occupy more niches, or the same niches in more parts of the world, than is the case today.

Oddly enough, even the unaggressive and secretive manatee can apparently displace the competition from certain environments. Daryl Domning, the world expert on sirenian evolution, paleontology, and paleoecology, has described sirenian occupancy of the Caribbean basin and has remarked on the "coevolution" of sirenians and seagrasses in that area. It is obvious that up until the early Pliocene epoch (about 5 million years ago) the dominant sirenians in the Caribbean were various types of dugongids. They developed specializations, such as tusks of different sizes and shapes, which allowed them to feed effectively on the various types of seagrasses that grew in that area. Between 2 and 5 million years ago, however, manatees and manatee-like sirenians inhabited both the Caribbean and the Amazon River basin. Domning speculates that the invasion of the Caribbean by manatees helped precipitate the demise of the dugongids there, in part at least because the manatees possessed dentition (teeth) that allowed them to be more effective foragers on the seagrasses.

The three living species of manatees arose from the animals that existed in the Caribbean and the Amazon River basin during the Pliocene. The morphologically similar West Indian manatee (which includes the Florida and

Antillean subspecies) and West African manatee are thought to have arisen from the Caribbean stock, whereas the distinctive-appearing Amazonian manatee probably arose from ancestors residing in the Amazon basin long ago. Manatees are known to have occupied Florida's waters at least since the Pleistocene, 1.5 to 1.1 million years ago.

The traits that unite the members of the Sirenia are several, and they reflect, as one might guess, both their heritage and their environment. As with other marine mammals, sirenians are very large: the West Indian manatee is the largest living sirenian, with individuals approaching 3,600 pounds (1,600 kilograms) in weight, but extinct sirenians such as the Steller's sea cow exceeded 26 feet (8 meters) in length and may have weighed as much as 10 tons (9,090 kilograms). Large size provides several advantages (and disadvantages, depending on the conditions under which a species lives). However, one very clear benefit for a mammal to be large when inhabiting an aquatic environment has to do with heat conservation. A large object (mammal or otherwise) has a relatively small surface area-to-volume ratio compared with a smaller object of similar shape; this means that there is relatively little surface across which to lose precious body heat. When one remembers that water conveys heat from a body about 25 times faster than air does, it becomes clear why the marine mammals, with their core body temperature similar to our own, evolved attributes like large size to help stay warm.

Large size is not the only feature shaped evolutionarily by an aquatic lifestyle. Manatees and other sirenians have evolved streamlined, spindle-shaped (fusiform) bodies that lack external protuberances that could cause drag. For example, the pelvic limbs (hind limbs) are absent (although vestiges of the pelvic bones exist deep in the muscles of sirenians), and pectoral limbs (front limbs, called flippers) have become reduced in size and shaped like paddles. For locomotion, the sirenians have powerful flukes that exist in two forms: a single, rounded fluke in the manatees, and split flukes (similar to those in a dolphin) in the dugongs. In terms of energetics, the use of a fluke for swimming, as opposed to the sorts of motions humans use, is extremely efficient and permits forward propulsion on both the upstroke and the downstroke. Sirenians can probably exceed 15 to 20 miles per hour in very short bursts—quite impressive, when one considers that the fastest swimming speed by a human is only slightly above 5 miles per hour.

Additional sirenian features include a lack of fur, having instead only sparse hairs on their bodies; lack of an externally distinct neck (another feature associated with streamlining); and their extremely heavy bones, which are both pachyostotic (thick or swollen) and osteosclerotic (hard and solid), a feature that facilitates staying on the bottom to feed. These are among the features that sirenians share as adaptations to their environment.

Adaptations associated with their herbivorous ancestry have also played a role in the features that unite the sirenians. All living species have specialized dentition (teeth) and horny plates in the mouth to help crush ingested plants; the extinct Steller's sea cow actually lacked teeth altogether. The lips of sirenians are enlarged (especially the upper lip) and are equipped with prehensile, as well as tactile, vibrissae; the size and flexibility of the lips facilitate manipulation (or more precisely "oripulation") of food. In addition, the brains of sirenians are not large, and herbivores tend to have smaller brains than do carnivores of the same body size.

Herbivores tend to have expanded areas of their digestive systems that function as fermentation vats for the breakdown of cellulose. In cattle and sheep, the "vats" exist as multiple stomachs, one of which is called the *rumen;* since stomachs occur in the initial part of the digestive system, such animals are called *foregut digesters* or *ruminants.* In contrast, the fermentation vat in horses and some other herbivorous mammals is the large intestine, the last major section of the digestive system before waste products exit the body. Horses are considered *hindgut digesters.*

The two digestive strategies have some striking similarities and differences. Both rely on a flourishing population of microbes in the guts to break down the cellulose that constitutes such a prominent component of plant bio-mass—after all, mammals lack the digestive enzymes to break down cellu-lose, so a symbiotic relationship with organisms that possess those enzymes is vital for mammalian herbivores. The rewards to the host (both ruminants and hindgut digesters) are the products of cellulose breakdown by the microbes; these products, called *volatile fatty acids,* are absorbed from the digestive sys-tem and nourish the host.

Ruminants accomplish cellulose breakdown (a process called *cellulolysis*) in their stomachs. There, ingested plant material is worked and reworked by the gut microbes. At times, small amounts of stomach contents are regurgitated into the mouth, where they are rechewed (what we call chewing cud) and mixed with saliva containing urea. By the time the stomach contents pass to the intestines, the plant materials have been thoroughly broken down and vir-tually all of the nutrients taken from them.

In contrast, horses and other hindgut digesters cannot regurgitate materi-als from their intestines. Plant materials are not held long in the digestive tract of the hindgut digesters, relative to the length of time food is retained in the stomachs of the ruminants. In the hindgut digesters, the plant materials tend to be incompletely broken down by the time they are excreted as wastes from the body.

Hindgut digesters are not nearly as efficient as the ruminants at extracting nutrients from food. This lack of efficiency has two clear behavioral and physi-ological consequences: hindgut digesters must constantly take in food, *but* hindgut digesters can survive on forage of such low quality that a ruminant eating it would starve.

Sirenians evolved from and are hindgut digesters—they eat "all the time," that is to say they may spend eight hours or more feeding each day. Seagrasses and other aquatic plants are not exceptionally nutritious, but that isn't really a concern for hindgut digesters. They just keep eating!

The large intestines of sirenians are enlarged fermentation vats that achieve astounding dimensions (that is, measure over 20 meters [66 feet] long and weigh, with contents, in the neighborhood of 70 kilograms [150 pounds]) and represent an impressive 14 percent of the body weight. My colleague, anatomist extraordinaire Sentiel "Butch" Rommel, and I have noticed something else besides how large the hindgut is: we have noticed that it is relatively larger in some sirenians than in others, and we think we know why.

Manatees and presumably dugongs have extremely low metabolic rates. In at least some manatees, the metabolic rate is about 15–20 percent of what scientists would expect based on body size. Especially in Florida, where temperatures of the water manatees occupy may be 40–50° Fahrenheit lower than manatee core body temperature, staying warm is a notable challenge for the manatee.

A by-product of cellulolysis is heat. Rommel and I have noted that manatees in Florida have much greater girth abdominally than do manatees of the same species in Central America. This is the case even for manatees for which body length and blubber thicknesses are equal—Florida manatees just tend to be bigger around than their more tropical cousins. We intend to investigate heat production and loss in manatees, and we speculate that the Florida manatees have, through natural selection, acquired larger cellulose fermentation vats (namely the large intestines) than their warm-water relatives possess, simply as an adaptation to staying warm.[1]

Manatees and their relatives represent unusual collections of adaptations. As the only living marine mammals that are also herbivores, they have been shaped for several tens of millions of years in ways that no other mammals have. Given the constraints imposed by both their herbivorous ancestry and an environment dramatically different from that of their ancestors, they have become an especially unusual group.

Living and Recent Sirenians

As noted, there are two primary groups of living and recent sirenians. The manatees (Family Trichechidae) are represented by three living species, whereas the dugong is the only living member of the Family Dugongidae. The Steller's sea cow, wiped out in 1768, only 27 years after its discovery by Russian explorers, was also a member of the Family Dugongidae (see table 2).

The manatees collectively are distinguishable from the dugongs by a number of features. Manatees have a rounded fluke rather than split flukes. Manatees exhibit horizontal replacement of their molariform (grinding) teeth throughout their lifetimes, which means that they have an apparently limitless supply of teeth. In contrast, dugongs have in their lifetimes a finite number of grinding teeth: three molars and three premolars in each quadrant of the jaws. The premolars and first molars are lost as the animal ages, whereas the remaining two molars grow throughout the life of the animal but become worn down at the surface. The presence of new teeth throughout life gives manatees a potential selective advantage over dugongs when it comes to eating gritty, abrasive vegetation that can wear teeth down over time. In addi-

Table 2. Species of manatees and dugongids.[a]

Family Trichechidae: manatees	
Trichechus manatus	West Indian manatee
Trichechus manatus manatus	Antillean manatee
Trichechus manatus latirostris	Florida manatee
Trichechus senegalensis	West African manatee
Trichechus inunguis	Amazonian manatee
Family Dugongidae: dugong and Steller's sea cow	
Dugong dugon	Dugong
Hydrodamalis gigas	Steller's sea cow

[a]Listed above are the three living species of manatees and the one surviving dugongid species. The other listed species, Steller's sea cow, is extinct. The sirenians were much more diverse millions of years ago.

tion, dugongs possess tusks (elongated upper incisor teeth that typically erupt from the gums only in males), which manatees lack.

Teeth are obviously related to feeding; so is the general makeup of the skull. In dugongs the rostrum (the anterior, or front, end of the skull) is sharply downturned as an adaptation to facilitate dugongs' feeding on the bottom. In contrast, the skulls of the various manatees are much less downturned, reflecting that these species are not restricted to being bottom feeders, but instead can easily feed on plants located virtually anywhere in the water column.

With this general information about sirenians in mind, it might be helpful to briefly examine information and issues associated with each species.

The West Indian Manatee: *Trichechus manatus*

The Florida Manatee: *Trichechus manatus latirostris*

The sirenian about which we know the most is the Florida manatee, thanks, in part, to some comprehensive research programs established nearly 30 years ago by members of the Sirenia Project (originally part of the U.S. Fish and Wildlife Service and currently administered by the Biological Resources Division of the U.S. Geological Survey) and Daniel K. Odell at the University of Miami. Both of these multifaceted programs benefited from studies by Joseph C. Moore and Daniel "Woody" Hartman in the 1950s and 1960s, respectively. Today, the State of Florida's Fish and Wildlife Conservation Commission conducts and/or supports more research on manatees than does any other group, but long-term partnerships and individual efforts deserve commendation for making the Florida manatee one of the best-studied marine mammals in the world.

The Florida manatee is the focus of this book, so I shall leave some details of its biology for other chapters. For comparisons with the other sirenians, however, it may be useful to have a few facts and figures close at hand.

Florida manatees are found year-round in coastal and riverine waters of peninsular Florida, with approximately equal numbers on the Atlantic and Gulf coasts of the state. Their inability to deal well with cold temperatures presents a real limitation on the habitats that manatees can occupy. In the summer, as water and air temperatures rise, manatees nomadically wander into waters of Georgia and the Carolinas, as well as into northern Gulf of Mexico waters along the Alabama, Mississippi, Louisiana, and Texas coasts. Of course, there are "outliers" such as the redoubtable male, Chessie, who ventured as far north as Rhode Island in summer 1996, and a few manatees that have taken up residency in the Bahamas, where sightings of manatees in the mid-1970s were rare enough to be a cause for local concern about invading "sea monsters."

During winter, manatee habitat is largely determined by the availability of warm water; most of the summer nomads move to natural and artificial sources of warm water provided by springs and power plants when it gets cold. What constitutes "cold" to a manatee? There is not a single temperature that provides a trigger for initiation of cold stress to manatees. Just as some humans tolerate cold better than others, some manatees appear to do so as well. And just as humans acclimate to cold as winter wears on, making them more and more comfortable with cooler temperatures, so, apparently, do manatees. Nonetheless, there is evidence, based on measurements of metabolic rates of manatees, that prolonged exposure to water temperatures below about 17–18° Celsius (about 63–65° Fahrenheit) can thermally stress manatees. For short durations, manatees appear to be able to tolerate water temperatures a few degrees colder.

In terms of adaptations to cold, manatees do several things. First, as has already been mentioned, they are large and they possess voluminous internal furnaces, powered by breakdown of cellulose by microbes in the large intestine. In addition, Florida manatees are well known for their tendency to seek warm-water refuges such as natural springs and industrial discharges when the weather turns cold. There are over two dozen known warm-water aggregation sites for manatees in winter; some may harbor just a few individuals, but several well-studied warm-water sources each shelter a significant percentage of the state's manatee population. I and others have counted over 300 manatees on cold days at each of several different locations around the state: the headwaters of Crystal River (the site of many of the photographs in this book) and power plants located near Tampa, Titusville, Riviera Beach, and Fort Myers. In fact, manatees have shown great ability to locate new or improved sources of warm water in winter. The recent "repowering" of an old power plant in Fort Lauderdale has led to that plant's producing much more warm water now than it did in the past, and more than 150 manatees may now be found using that more abundant resource on cold winter days; prior to the repowering, only a dozen or so manatees used the area on cold days.

However, on the other side of the coin, flow rates at some springs critical to manatees in winter, such as Blue Spring in northeastern Florida, have experienced significant reductions due, presumably, to a combination of effects of droughts and dramatically increased tapping of the aquifer for human uses. In addition, possible changes in the power industry associated with deregulation or with the availability of less costly alternatives to produce power may reduce or eliminate some industrial refuges manatees need to survive. Changes in availability of warm water, and resultant consequences to manatees, are among the most critical issues facing managers for that species at the start of the twenty-first century.

Whether at the warm-water refuges or not, manatees that are cold may bask at the surface on sunny days. Their dark skin absorbs heat and helps them avoid thermal stress. Floating, as it turns out, is easy for manatees despite their dense, heavy bones and skin. Manatee lungs stretch virtually the length of the body cavity, just alongside the backbone. In addition, manatee digestive processes produce a lot of gas in the intestines. Butch Rommel and I have considered and written about buoyancy in manatees, and we think the stout diaphragm is positioned in a way that compresses the intestines and the gas therein, permitting an animal to adjust its buoyancy without expending lots of energy. Flatulence, believe it or not, may contribute to buoyancy control! Isn't it remarkable (and hopefully interesting) that anatomical adaptations for one presumed function (such as buoyancy control) have profound implications for other biological functions (such as thermoregulation)?

Rather surprising to many people, manatees have relatively high thermal conductance across their surfaces compared to other marine mammals. That is, they can lose heat relatively easily due to the arrangement and thickness of their blubber layers. On the other hand, manatees possess sophisticated vascular adaptations that reduce the extent to which warm arterial blood, departing from the core of the body, loses that warmth when it reaches cooler parts of the body near the skin. These adaptations help manatees retain heat.

Interestingly enough, certain internal regions of the body cannot tolerate high temperatures. For example, sperm viability is reduced when testicular temperature rises; developmental defects may occur when uterine temperatures are high; and nervous system function is impaired when temperature exceeds normal levels. How do manatees keep such areas relatively cool, when their bodies seem to be adapted for heat retention? The answer lies in vascular shunts that permit cooler blood returning from near the skin to return directly to those organs that need to stay cool.

Manatees may be described as *euryhaline,* which means that they can occupy fresh water and seawater, and anything in between. Scientists have speculated about manatees' physiological need to drink fresh water. The structure of the kidney suggests that manatees should be able to deal with the "salt load" that drinking seawater or eating salty vegetation would impose; however, it is still uncertain whether manatees need periodic access to fresh water, and, if so, with what frequency. The truth is that they seek fresh water, whether they require it or not. Tom O'Shea, the former leader of the Sirenia Project, is fond of saying that manatees and fresh water remind him of kids and ice cream: they may not need it, but they surely do like it! Manatees enjoy a drink of fresh water enough that a common lure used by scientists to capture manatees for study is simply a running hose, dangling above the surface of the water.

Manatees commonly occur in shallow waters, where vegetation for food is abundant. However, it is not unusual to find manatees in extremely shallow water and even partially hauled out on land to feed. As good hindgut digesters, manatees eat a lot and they eat almost anything; as I used to tell my students, if something is green and cannot swim very fast, manatees probably eat it! It would be a mistake to think of manatees as finicky eaters, although it is interesting that they do avoid a few plants, such as blue-green algae, that contain natural toxins.

Although the diet of manatees includes several dozen species of submerged, floating, emergent, and shoreline plants, in salt water the animals feed primarily on seagrasses including turtle grass (*Thalassia testudinum*), shoal grass (*Halodule wrightii*), and the appropriately named manatee grass (*Syringodium filiforme*). Manatees along the coasts may also consume mangrove seedlings and leaves, as well as a variety of red, green, and brown algae.

In freshwater rivers and canals, a variety of native plants (for example, *Vallisneria, Potamogeton,* and *Cabomba*) find their way into the mouths (and stomachs) of manatees, but a major part of the diet in some parts of the state turns out to be exotic (introduced) species such as the water hyacinth (*Eichhornia crassipes*) and hydrilla (*Hydrilla verticillata*). These plants have invaded and taken over many Florida waterways, outcompeting and eliminating the native aquatic plants and proliferating to an extent where they block waterways and cost millions of dollars to (unsuccessfully!) control each year. In an ill-fated experiment in 1964–66, eight manatees were captured by scientists associated with Florida Atlantic University and placed in weed-choked canals to see whether the animals could keep the plants under control. Unfortunately, cold weather and vandals ended both the experiment and the lives of several of the manatees.

In contrast, in Georgetown, Guyana, manatees (in this case the Antillean manatee) have been used since 1952 to keep canals and a lake clear of infesting weed growth. Between 1954 and 1974, over 200 manatees were captured and placed in the canal system, a major effort to be sure, but one that bore effective and cost-effective results in terms of weed clearance.

People who study wildlife (including scientists, naturalists, hunters, and others) know of a phenomenon in which mammals residing in cold climates tend to be larger in size than members of the same or closely related species in warmer areas; compare, for example, robust whitetail deer in Minnesota with those dainty individuals in Florida. This phenomenon is called Bergmann's Rule by scientists, and it seems to apply to manatees as well. Thus, the largest living manatees are found in Florida, the coolest region of the world in which manatees are found.

Manatees in Florida routinely exceed 3 meters (10 feet) in length and top a ton in weight. An examination of the photographs in this book allows readers to understand what manatees look like better than any words could: enormous, streamlined beasts, with rough skin, nails on the ends of their paddle-like flippers, powerful flukes, and bulbous, bewhiskered faces.

They can each consume several tens of pounds (some possibly unrealistic estimates suggest up to 200 pounds [91 kilograms]) of vegetation each day. Thus, even though manatees may not be abundant relative to most other species in Florida (currently the manatee population is probably somewhere in the range of 3,500 individuals), they may have a significant impact on productivity and nutrient cycling, especially when they are aggregated in the vicinity of artificial and natural warm-water refuges during cold weather.

The precise role that manatees play in seagrass ecosystems is still somewhat unclear. The dugong has been described as a "cultivation grazer" whose cropping exerts a positive effect on seagrass productivity. Perhaps a useful analogy involves lawns and lawn mowing: if you don't mow (crop) your lawn, its growth (productivity) slows considerably. Regular mowing (cropping) just makes the grass grow faster.

Manatees crop seagrass leaves, although they also root out rhizomes. It is possible—even probable—that the cropping of seagrasses and other vegetation by manatees may promote greater productivity, and even greater plant diversity, in local areas. This increase in productivity, in turn, has multiple benefits including promoting larger stocks of fishes and better fishing.

In his provocative and insightful essay entitled "Why Save the Manatee?" Daryl Domning noted the often-unacknowledged ecological importance of manatees in Florida. As I will discuss in chapter 7, Domning also noted that despite the importance of their ecological role, there are even more important reasons to save manatees.

The Antillean Manatee: *Trichechus manatus manatus*

The Antillean manatee occupies a large but discontinuous range, extending from well south of the equator in Brazil all the way north into Mexico and even southern Texas, and including Caribbean islands such as Cuba, Hispaniola, Jamaica, and Puerto Rico. The Antillean manatee resembles its northern cousin, the Florida manatee, in many ways. However, there are some important biological and ecological differences between the two subspecies, as well as some different conservation issues.

Externally, Antillean manatees are similar to Florida manatees, except that the latter subspecies tends to be a little longer and much heavier, as noted above. The two subspecies have been differentiated primarily by their distribution and through extensive analysis of their cranial (skull) anatomy. Lately, genetic analyses have reinforced the subspecific status. Perhaps the most obvious biological difference between the two subspecies is that the annual distribution of Florida manatees is governed to a large degree by cold, whereas the distribution of Antillean manatees in many parts of their range is governed by wet-dry seasons and by hunting pressure.

Antillean manatees exhibit a rather patchy distribution along the coasts, taking advantage of locations with abundant vegetation to eat and fresh water to drink. In the wet season, manatees may be found up rivers where the currents are not too strong. In the dry season, they move downstream when water levels in the rivers drop. At certain times of year, environmental factors may concentrate manatees in particular locations, making them especially susceptible to hunting by human hunters and possibly by predators.

As I will discuss later, management and conservation of manatees in Florida is a challenge; imagine, however, trying to effectively conserve a species whose range crosses the borders of 21 different countries, each with its own set of laws, customs, and economic, social, political, and conservation issues. In a few countries, such as Mexico, Belize, and Guatemala, specially protected areas for manatees have been created, but lack of enforcement limits the effectiveness of such areas. Couple the persistence of hunting pressure and the small size of the manatee population in most countries with very low levels of funding, and conservation becomes a daunting task. People such as Benjamin Morales-Vela, Ruby Montoya, Tony Mignucci, Nicole Auil, and James Powell (to name a few) deserve a lot of credit for doing what they have. And in some cases what they have accomplished is pretty remarkable—witness the creation by the Mexican government of a manatee sanctuary in Chetumal Bay, promoted by the research done by Benjamin Morales-Vela. The conservation status of Antillean manatees appears in table 3.

There are over 3,000 Florida manatees. Scientists do not have a clear idea of the number of Antillean manatees that are present in most countries. Possibly the best data come from Belize and Mexico, where a number of scientists have counted manatees or conducted other research. In 1989, Tom O'Shea and Lex Salisbury called Belize "one of the last strongholds" for manatees in Central America;[2] the most recent aerial survey counts sighted over 250

Table 3. The status of the various sirenians according to selected laws and conventions.

Species	CITES	ESA	IUCN[a]
Florida manatee	Appendix I[b]	Endangered	Vulnerable
Antillean manatee	Appendix I[b]	Endangered	Vulnerable
West African manatee[c]	Appendix II[d]	Threatened	Vulnerable
Amazonian manatee	Appendix I[b]	Endangered	Vulnerable
Dugong	Appendix I[e]	Endangered	Vulnerable
Steller's sea cow	—	Extinct	—

[a]CITES stands for the Convention on International Trade in Endangered Species of Wild Flora and Fauna; ESA stands for the U.S. Endangered Species Act; and IUCN stands for the International Union for the Conservation of Nature and Natural Resources (now called the World Conservation Union). Sirenians are protected by national legislation in all countries they occupy.

[b]Appendix I corresponds to the highest level of concern and protection.

[c]West African manatees are also protected under Class A, African Convention for the Conservation of Nature and Natural Resources.

[d]Appendix II corresponds to the second highest level of concern and protection.

[e]Dugongs are listed under Appendix I except in Australia, where they are listed under Appendix II.

manatees along the corridor between southeastern Mexico (Quintana Roo state) and Belize. To put that number in context, I regularly see more manatees than that at each of several power plant discharges in Florida on a cold day.

For a country-by-country description of the status of Antillean manatees, I refer readers to excellent publications by Lynn Lefebvre (current leader of the Sirenia Project) and her colleagues or to J. E. Reynolds III and D. K. Odell's *Manatees and Dugongs*.

The West African Manatee:

Trichechus senegalensis

The size, appearance, and habitat of the West African manatee are quite similar to those of the West Indian manatee. A close look at the face of the West African manatee shows that it has a blunter snout and more protuberant eyes than its New World relative. West African manatees are also a bit more slender than are West Indian manatees. Other than that, the two species are quite similar in appearance.

As described for Antillean manatees, the distribution of the West African species seems to be affected by wet and dry seasons. For manatees located well inland in Africa, lakes may be the only adequate source of water during the dry times. And as occurs for Antillean manatees, when manatees in Africa become concentrated, they become particularly vulnerable targets for hunters. Similar to the other manatee species, natural predation levels appear low; anecdotal accounts here and around the world suggest that, on rare occasions, a manatee may be killed by a shark or crocodilian.

The distribution of West African manatees is even more extensive than that of Antillean manatees, at least in terms of the number of countries occupied. West African manatees inhabit coastal waters and rivers and lakes of almost two dozen countries, from Senegal in the north to Angola in the south. They exist in the upper reaches of the Niger River to Guinea and through the inland delta of Mali, although manatees in the upper Niger cannot reach the sea due to the presence of hydroelectric dams and cataracts downstream. Similarly, manatees inhabit two tributaries of Lake Chad (but apparently not the lake itself), and these rivers (the Logone and the Chari) do not generally communicate with the sea.

Scientists have no real idea of the number of West African manatees. In many countries, hunting of manatees is common either for food or to reduce the extent to which the animals become entangled in and tear fishing nets, destroy fish that have been netted, or plunder rice fields. On the other hand, in a few countries tribal legends, customs, and superstitions protect manatees, which are sometimes referred to as a water deity, called *mammy wata,* by locals. In the Korup region of Cameroon, for example, people simply have never developed a taste for manatee meat, so the animals remain unhunted there.

Due to lack of knowledge, hunting pressure, habitat modification and destruction, warfare, political instability, and the fact that effective conservation of manatees will require a unified effort by a number of countries that do not necessarily get along, the welfare of West African manatees is very uncertain. West African manatees are protected under a variety of laws and international conventions (table 3). However, as in other parts of the world, despite their legal protection (on paper), manatee survival is tenuous because enforcement of the conservation legislation is difficult and inconsistent. It is extremely encouraging, though, that in a number of countries, grassroots efforts are emerging to study and conserve manatees, and several countries (for example Ivory Coast, Nigeria, and Cameroon) have created specially protected manatee reserves and sanctuaries. Many of these programs owe their genesis to James Powell, who spent several years in the 1980s in Ivory Coast, Senegal, Cameroon, and other countries, where he did research, trained assistants, and motivated further study. In Ivory Coast, Gambia, and Ghana, for example, new and energetic scientists are emerging who may well make a difference.

The Amazonian Manatee:
Trichechus inunguis

The smallest of the manatees, the Amazonian species is distinctive in other ways as well. Rarely exceeding 3 meters in length or 500 kilograms in weight, this species is easy to distinguish due to its smooth "rubbery" skin, long pectoral flippers, lack of nails (hence the species name *inunguis*) at the ends of the flippers, and the frequent presence of white or pink belly patches.

Amazonian manatees may be found throughout the drainage of the Amazon River and its tributaries in Brazil, Peru, Colombia, and Ecuador. Amazonian manatees are the only sirenians confined to freshwater habitats. More, perhaps, than the other manatees, Amazonian manatees are affected by the dry season. At such times, manatees occupy deep lakes, which lack bottom vegetation due to their depth and murkiness. As water levels drop, manatees are unable to reach overhanging vegetation either. Scientists have estimated that Amazonian manatees may fast during the dry season for as many as 200 days!

Nor is lack of food the only problem for Amazonian manatees during the dry season. Hunters take advantage of the animals' concentration in one spot, with little place to hide; jaguars, too, prey on manatees aggregated in lakes. Manatees are not simply hunted by local people for food and other products. In Ecuador, for example, military personnel patrolling the borders have been reported to kill and consume manatees regularly.

Given their remote habitat, it is not surprising that manatees in the Amazon are not as well studied as are manatees in Florida and certain other parts of the world. Scientists don't even have a real idea of how many exist. However, long-term research and conservation programs at Manaus and Tefé, both in Brazil, have been conducted under the leadership of people like Vera da Silva, Miriam Marmontel, and the late Robin Best. The Projeto Peixe-Boi (Brazilian Manatee Project) was initiated in 1975 in Manaus and continues to be an important center for research, education, and conservation work for manatees. And in Brazil and Peru, huge protected areas have been created that should help conserve the species. Amazonian manatees, like the other sirenians, are protected by both national and international laws and agreements (table 3).

The biggest threat to the Amazonian manatee, now and in the future, stems from staggering assaults on the ecosystem. A number of authors have documented the impacts to species and habitat, and the figures are breathtaking (almost enough to make Florida's losses seem trivial): for example, deforestation in Latin America destroyed 7.4 million hectares (Brazil alone eliminated 3.2 million hectares) of tropical forest per year through the 1980s, contributing to the extinction of perhaps 10,000 forest species per year. Mining, oil drilling, lumber industries, and hunting continue to affect manatees and other species—perhaps eventually to extinction.

The Dugong:

Dugong dugon

The dugong has been quite well studied thanks to the efforts of scientists such as Helene Marsh, Paul Anderson, Tony Preen, and George Heinsohn in Australia; Brydget Hudson in Papua New Guinea; Vic Cockcroft in East Africa; and Hans de Iongh in Indonesia, to name a few. In some regards, scientific studies of dugongs in Australia paved the way for similar sorts of studies on manatees in Florida. For example, Marsh and her colleagues took advantage of the fact that aboriginal hunters continue to hunt dugongs for subsistence purposes; by developing ties with local hunters, the scientists were able relatively easily to gather information on anatomy, reproductive biology, and life history of dugongs. Furthermore, the animals that were harvested by hunters were presumably healthy animals that could be examined soon after death, making anatomical and histological (microscopic anatomy) studies much more effective than is the case when carcasses (possibly resulting from diseases) are recovered after a day or two in the sun.

Dugongs are shorter and more slender than are the manatees, with the possible exception of the Amazonian manatee. Like the latter, dugongs have smooth skin, but unlike any other living sirenians, dugongs possess tusks and split flukes. Dugongs occupy coastal waters where predators such as large sharks and killer whales have been observed to succeed occasionally in making a meal of one.

Although research projects on Australian dugongs have been plentiful, the same cannot be said for most dugong populations around the world. The species has an enormous range (from Okinawa and other east Asian locations, past Australia, New Guinea, and other Pacific islands, to India and Sri Lanka, into the Red Sea and the Arabian Gulf, and all the way to East Africa) that includes at least 37 countries and territories, between about 26° north and 26° south of the equator. The worldwide population of dugongs is probably in the several tens of thousands, but in most countries only small, vulnerable, isolated, relict populations of dugongs have survived hunting pressure and habitat loss. Only in a few places is the status of the species well known and reasonably secure (table 3). And even in locations like the Queensland coast of Australia where dugong populations have been in reasonable shape, the combination of environmental stresses (such as cyclones that lead to eradication of seagrass beds) and coastal development provides little reassurance that the dugong is secure for the long run.

Dugongs are almost exclusively marine. They are also almost exclusively bottom feeders, a behavior mandated by the tremendous downward deflection of the front of the skull. These factors mean that the dugong is more parochial in its habitat needs than are some of the manatee species. This lack of flexibility has important conservation implications.

So does the fact that studies of life history of the dugong suggest that this species may have a lower reproductive potential than do the manatees. Female dugongs may not reach sexual maturity until the age of 18 years, and the youngest age at which females reach sexual maturity in certain locations in Queensland, Australia, and Papua New Guinea is 10–14.5 years. Interbirth intervals in dugongs are generally similar to those reported for Florida manatees (that is, one calf every 2.5 to 3 years), but may extend for two to three times that length of time. Dugongs may live as long as 73 years, which compares to the maximum recorded lifespan in manatees of 59 years.

Their life history attributes biologically limit the rate at which dugong populations can grow. Helene Marsh has suggested that it is unlikely that any dugong population could increase at a rate exceeding 5 percent, even under optimal conditions. This rate of increase makes dugongs extremely vulnerable to over-exploitation—more than is the case for manatees.

Scientists have documented that a variety of human factors impact dugongs around the world. These impacts include habitat destruction (especially destruction of seagrasses associated with dredging, land development, and land reclamation), entanglement in fishing nets and traps, entanglement in nets placed around beaches to protect swimmers from sharks, deliberate hunting for subsistence, and strikes by vessels. It is worth noting that, in many countries where dugongs are found, pressures derived from unprecedented (and continuing) growth of the human population jeopardize the long-term existence of many living resources, not just dugongs.

Marsh and her colleagues recently completed a comprehensive document entitled *The Dugong (*Dugong dugon*). Status Reports and Action Plans for Countries and Territories in Its Range* for the World Conservation Union, the United Nations Environment Programme, the World Conservation Monitoring Centre, and the CRC Reef Research Centre. The document carefully describes the status of dugongs around the world and provides solid, country- or territory-specific recommendations for dugong conservation.

Steller's Sea Cow:

Hydrodamalis gigas

Occupying cold, subarctic waters in the Bering Sea, Steller's sea cow was unique among the Recent sirenians: it lacked teeth, apparently could not dive, lacked "finger bones," and reached more immense proportions than has any other sirenian species. It also warrants notice as a tragic "poster child" representing human misuse and overexploitation of a resource.

The sea cow was discovered in November 1741, when the Russian brig *St. Peter* became wrecked near the Aleutian Islands. The captain of the ship was a Dane, Vitus Bering, for whom the Bering Sea is named. Bering and his crew were charged with exploring that area and claiming land and other resources for Russia.

Bering and some of his crew perished following the shipwreck during the harsh subarctic winter, but most of the men survived, in part due to the presence of the gigantic sea cow. Defenseless and easy to capture since it could not dive, the sea cow was pretty easy prey for the hungry men, and one kill could feed many people. One of the beneficiaries was a young German crew member, the naturalist Georg Wilhelm Steller, who recorded most of what we know about the behavior, appearance, and hunting of the sea cow that now bears his name.

Ultimately the crew used salvageable parts of the *St. Peter* to construct a new, smaller vessel that took them home. But they returned to Russia with stories of great riches such as otter and fur seal pelts and copper . . . and stories of how easy it was to live off the meat of sea cows. Subsequent voyages took advantage of both the natural wealth of the area and of the sea cows for food. According to the naturalist Leonhard Stejneger, from about 1743 "until 1763 hardly a winter passed without one or more parties spending eight or nine months in hunting fur-animals there, during which time the crews lived almost exclusively on the meat of the sea-cow."[3]

Stejneger estimated that perhaps 2,000 Steller's sea cows existed when the species was discovered by Bering and his crew. That small number of presumably slow-breeding animals simply could not withstand the losses imposed year after year by hunters' appetites. By 1768, only 27 years after it was discovered, Steller's sea cow no longer existed.

Vulnerable Giants

chapter 3

Biological Constraints of Nature— Assisted by People

FOR AN INTELLIGENT SPECIES, humans sometimes make assumptions that don't necessarily make a lot of sense. This has been true, unfortunately, of the way we have harvested or otherwise affected many species of wildlife. It may be useful when considering the status, adaptations, and management of manatees in Florida to have as a context or background some information regarding those same topics for other species and other times.

Back in the eighteenth and nineteenth centuries, the harvest of marine mammals and many other species was constrained only by the abilities and skills of the hunters themselves. People simply didn't seem to be concerned about the possibility of wiping out the cash cows on which their livelihood depended. Why was that?

When pelagic whalers started to exploit species around the globe, they were struck by the apparently limitless supply of resources they encountered. Presumably it rarely, if ever, entered their consciousness that they might, somehow, wipe out certain species. Even if the thought did occur to them, two mitigating (but wrong!) ideas presumably followed closely: (1) living resources have no intrinsic value—they simply exist to be exploited by those ingenious and hardy enough to do so; and (2) marine mammals, in particular, were pretty clever, and if it appeared that their numbers were dropping, it was an illusion—the animals simply had moved to new areas to avoid persecution by the hunters.

By the late nineteenth century and the turn of the twentieth century, however, it was becoming apparent to a few scientists and even to the whalers and sealers, such as Captain Charles W. Scammon,[1] that a great many species of marine mammals were simply disappearing. Shortly after World War I, the U.S. pelagic whaling fleet had disappeared, not so much because people were terribly concerned about the welfare of the whales, but because it was no longer economically feasible to earn a good living hunting them.

Nearly 100 years later, certain species of whales have not recovered; they hover on the brink of extinction. The North Atlantic right whale (*Balaena glacialis*), for example, numbers only about 300 individuals, despite almost a century of protection, at least on paper. Thus the overharvest of certain species can have long-lasting, even permanent, effects. What factors contribute to such a dismal prognosis?

In our anthropocentric world, we tend to focus on issues, both good and bad, related to people. Certainly one cannot shrug off environmental concerns relating to a burgeoning worldwide human population of nearly 7 billion. But it is a mistake to overlook the fact that some species just are not able to breed very quickly or to recover from reductions in their numbers very well. These species are sometimes referred to in ecological terms as *K-strategists*, a term suggesting that they have developed suites of anatomical, physiological, and behavioral adaptations or attributes that permit them to maintain relatively stable populations that hover at or near the carrying capacity (denoted by ecologists as K) of their environment. The right whale elegantly exemplifies a K-strategist. Among other things, K-strategists may be gigantic in size, have very long life-spans, physically develop and reach sexual maturity slowly, produce small litters, breed numerous times in their lives (called *iteroparity*), provide long and extensive parental care for their few offspring, have strong and prolonged social bonds, and generally are relatively poor colonizers of new habitats.

The K-strategists exist at one end of a gradient of what are termed *life history strategies;*[2] at the other end of the gradient are the so-called *r-strategists.* The letter *r* is used by ecologists to indicate the intrinsic rate of increase for a population or species, and the r-strategists of the world are endowed with adaptations that facilitate rapid population growth. A pink shrimp (*Penaeus duorarum*), for example, provides a good model for an r-strategist. This species and other r-strategists are relatively small (let's face it, they're shrimps); have short lives; mature quickly; produce huge numbers of offspring (for some species, into the millions per adult female) that are provided little or no parental care and for which mortality is enormous; generally only breed once in their lives (that is, are *semelparous*); are plastic in their behaviors and are able to colonize, even dominate, new habitats well; and have few, if any, lasting social bonds.

Most species, of course, lie somewhere along the gradient between the two poles provided by the consummate r-strategists and the exemplary K-strategists. Consider a domestic cat, for example: clearly cats represent some "middle ground" of adaptations between those of the right whale and those of the pink shrimp. So do manatees, although they, like all of the marine mammals, are much displaced toward the K-strategist pole.

Before considering the life history strategies and population status of manatees, it may be useful to pause and ask: Why do life history strategies really matter?

This chapter opened with the idea that humans have an unenviable history of managing resources poorly. Over 40 percent of the fisheries in the United States are jeopardized by the fact that they have overharvested the species on which they base their livelihood. Part of the (repeated) problem is that people may fail to recognize that different species have different adaptations that lead to different abilities to reproduce and to recover from harvest; in the absence of such recognition, people, including managers, have often made nonconservative assumptions that have jeopardized both species and livelihoods.

For example, traditional approaches to commercial fishing have been based on assumptions that reproductive potential (or fecundity) of species being harvested was high. Reconsider the pink shrimp mentioned above: if pink shrimp were inadvertently overharvested one year, but the habitat necessary for successful breeding and growth and survival of young was left intact, the extremely high fecundity of the females could replenish the population size in a relatively short time, provided that overharvest was not perpetuated. On the other hand, an adult female right whale may only produce one calf every four to six years; if right whales (especially sexually mature females) were inadvertently overharvested, even under optimal conditions, it would be *biologically impossible* to regenerate the population in a short period of time. At times when right whale numbers become reduced, it would be possible for fast-breeding (more r-selected) competitors to "invade" and start to claim the niche of the right whale, further reducing the rate, or even the possibility, of right whale recovery. If high harvest levels persisted for some time after the inadvertent overharvest, right whales might well become reduced to so few animals that recovery time could take decades, if not centuries, even under the best of conditions. Unfortunately, that's where the species stands today.[3]

Thus models that assume high species fecundity and that are not conservative in allowing for occasional overharvest may condemn the K-strategists to having perpetually low numbers. Other assumptions also affect the recovery, or nonrecovery, of certain populations or species.

One of the more common assumptions involves the misperception that K (environmental carrying capacity) is a constant. Nothing could be further from the truth. Natural environmental variation affects carrying capacity; so does pollution, and so does harvest of non-target species. For example, when humans remove large numbers of certain species from an area, the remaining populations are not unaffected. Take wolves and mountain lions out of an area, and deer and rabbit populations skyrocket; harvest lots of deer and rabbits, and the wolves migrate or starve.

Even the "green" areas in our world are not really "natural." Eminent marine ecologist Paul Dayton of Scripps Institution of Oceanography and his colleagues have documented that even those marine and estuarine ecosystems that seem to be relatively pristine due to the presence of a lot of animals are actually far removed from what is "normal" due to changes brought about by human overfishing and other activities. As scientists today assess such ecosystems, what should they use as appropriate natural benchmarks of ecosystem health? And without such benchmarks, what should be the goals of conservation and of restoration?

Furthermore, in the face of significant changes in habitat and carrying capacity, species having which life history strategy are favored? The r-strategists, of course, may be expected to have an inside track to success because they tend to outbreed and outcompete the K-strategists and to be better, more adaptable colonizers.

In summary, one must tread cautiously and conservatively when either harvesting or trying to effect the recovery of the K-strategists of the world. The care and conservatism, in fact, need to extend *both* to the direct impacts to the species in question and to indirect impacts such as habitat destruction or modification. In the absence of such care, there are already a number of examples of strongly K-selected species (for example, cheetahs, North Atlantic right whales, rhinos, monk seals) that resist recovery, even in the face of current admirable intentions, dedicated scientists and conservationists, infusion of unprecedented amounts of funds for both science and management, and ample protective legislation.

Having identified some failures and risks, it is important to note that there are occasional success stories in terms of conservation and recovery of large mammals. The number of California gray whales (*Eschrichtius robustus*) was reduced in the 1800s by whalers to such extremely low levels that imminent extinction seemed a real possibility. But gray whales in the eastern North Pacific had recovered sufficiently (over 26,000 individuals) that in June 1994, the eastern stock of this species was removed from the Endangered Species List (although the western stock still exists at a perilously low population size—just 100 or so individuals). The dramatic recovery of northern elephant seals (*Mirounga angustirostris*) from a few tens of individuals in the late 1800s to over 50,000 animals today is also remarkable.

But such examples, unfortunately, represent exceptions rather than the rule, and there are danger signals that all is not well even for those species, such as northern elephant seals and eastern Pacific gray whales, that have demonstrated significant population increases and apparent recovery. The lesson is that, in management, one size definitely does not fit all. What may seem to work for a highly fecund fish or shellfish may spell extinction for a slow-breeding mammal. And even high fecundity cannot prevent overfishing or habitat destruction and modification from wreaking havoc on the status of a species—witness crashes in numbers of cod off New England and of ancho-veta off Peru. Management actions must be tailored to the needs and vulner-abilities of the species in question, and understanding and clarification of those criteria are part of what science provides.

Manatee Life History Facts and Figures

Twenty-five years ago, manatees worldwide were poorly studied, so their conservation and management needs could only be assumed. And as noted above, inappropriate and nonconservative assumptions can spell disaster in species management.

But scientists from a variety of agencies and organizations in the United States have attacked the deficiencies in our knowledge so rigorously for three decades that it seems fair to say that people know more today about Florida manatees than about most other marine mammal species in the world. There are, to be sure, gaps in our knowledge about certain key aspects of manatee biology (for instance, sensory biology, habitat selection mechanisms, genetics, aspects of reproductive biology). In part, this lack of knowledge is because much of the research done to date has been governed by what managers wanted or needed to know at the time to address specific questions or con-cerns, rather than by the optimal, broad-based scientific approach. It is also unfortunately true that some important databases commonly used to support management decisions remain unanalyzed because of staffing insufficiencies. Nonetheless, the point remains valid that we know a lot about manatees. A more important corollary is that, unlike the case for most other species or populations of marine mammals, lack of science is not a major restriction in managing manatees and manatee habitat.

As noted earlier in this chapter, manatees are K-strategists relative to the vast majority of species, although not as strongly so as are some other species of marine and terrestrial mammals (such as some whales and elephants). Let's consider the suite of adaptations associated with K-strategists to see exactly how manatees stack up.

The first hint that manatees are K-strategists involves their enormous body size. The largest manatee recorded weighed 1,620 kilograms (almost 3,600 pounds). Measurements exist that indicate manatees may exceed 4 meters (a little over 13 feet) in length. Of course, not all manatees reach such proportions, but adult manatees average 3 meters (almost 10 feet) long and 1,000 kilograms (2,200 pounds) in weight. Even newborn calves are sizeable, averaging 1.2 to 1.4 meters (4 to 4.5 feet) long and about 30 kilograms (66 pounds) in weight.

Scientists determine the age of a manatee by examining rings called growth-layer-groups found in the ear bones. The rings are deposited annually and can be counted much as one would count annual rings to assess the age of a fallen tree. As with trees, this technique works well for deceased manatees, but unlike trees (whose age, when living, can be determined by taking cores of the trunk) there are obvious limitations when trying to consider the age structure of the living population of manatees.

Counting the growth-layer-groups, the scientist who developed the technique, Miriam Marmontel of Brazil, determined that manatees can live at least as long as 59 years. That seems like a figure that would place manatees among the very most K-selected species in existence. Other data soften that picture.

One of my former students, Meghan Pitchford, has followed and refined Marmontel's approach and has determined the age of over 2,000 manatees that have been recovered in a carcass salvage network that has existed in Florida since 1974. Meg has not found any manatees older than 59, but she has noted that relatively few manatees reach even 30 years of age. In fact, the average age of the 2,000+ manatees for which Meg has determined the age is only 5.8 years old; this figure includes newborn animals, but even if one were to consider only the adult manatees for which age has been determined, the average age is only 12 years. In addition, Florida manatees achieve sexual maturity at a surprisingly young age for such gigantic mammals: male manatees may start producing sperm as young as 2 years of age, and females may become pregnant in their third year of life.

Let's put this information in context. Before the advent of modern medicine, humans lived about as long as manatees apparently can—that is, for a few decades. But people never, to the best of my knowledge, reached sexual maturity at 2 or 3 years old. The unexpectedly early onset of sexual maturity in manatees is quite a surprise, and it increases the reproductive potential of the species; it also suggests that manatees may be a little less K-selected than one might guess based on their size and potential longevity alone.

Reproductive potential also is influenced by factors other than age at sexual maturity. Litter size, for example, has already been shown to be an extremely important criterion. So is the interval between breeding periods. For manatees, a single calf per pregnancy is the norm, with twin fetuses being found during examination of carcasses in about 4 percent of the pregnancies; field studies have noted females accompanied by equal-sized calves presumed to be twins about 1–2 percent of the time. The intercalf interval has been estimated to average about 2.5 years, and gestation time is about 11–14 months. Scientists have noted that the intercalf interval can be several times the usual value of 2.5 years, presumably depending in part on the health of the female manatee. There has long been speculation that even a single severe wound resulting from a collision with a boat, or exposure to severe cold weather or a red tide bloom, may dramatically affect female health and reproductive potential. In fact, ongoing research by Cathy Walsh and Carl Luer of Mote Marine Laboratory suggests that the function of the immune system may be severely compromised for some time (weeks to months) in a manatee exposed to certain environmental stressors or trauma.

Once a calf is born, it spends a year or more with its mother, during which time it presumably learns locations of resources (warm water in winter, lush submerged aquatic vegetation to eat) necessary for survival. The calves quickly increase in size from a birth length and weight of a little over 1.0 meter (over 3 feet) and 30 kilograms (66 pounds), respectively, to a two-year-old length and weight that can exceed 2.5 meters (about 8 feet) and 250 kilograms (550 pounds), respectively. Although calves may remain in the same area as their mothers for several years, the period of nutritional dependence of the young is much shorter—on the order of a couple to a few months. It is not unusual for youngsters (referred to as juveniles) to be completely on their own by the time they are two years old.

Qualitatively, manatees appear to possess a mix of starkly K-selected attributes and surprisingly r-selected ones. The latter suggest that, given a chance, manatee populations have the potential to recover better than is the case for some other large mammals such as certain species of whales.

Life history data can be used in a more quantitative fashion in models to provide insights that are extremely relevant to managers and conservationists. For example, noted sirenian biologist and conservationist Helene Marsh, of James Cook University in Townsville, Australia, used life history data from manatees to calculate an annual percentage rate of increase *for stable populations* of manatees. She found that, if the mean age at which females give birth for the first time is four years, the interbirth interval dramatically affects the potential percentage rate of population increase: a 2.5-year intercalf interval (the usual figure), for example, could lead in a stable manatee population to a 6.6 percent annual increase in population size, whereas a 5-year interval (noted for some females) reduces the potential annual increase to a meager 1.9 percent.

Similarly, Marmontel and her coworkers used life history and other data to develop a population viability model for manatees in Florida. These authors determined that manatees in Florida would be driven to extinction in less than 1,000 years under certain plausible scenarios such as a 10 percent increase in adult mortality or a 10 percent decrease in fecundity. The period of 1,000 years may seem to be a long, long time, based on human history, but relative to the time manatees have resided in Florida waters (well over one million years), it seems rather fleeting. With clearly documented increases in mortality of Florida manatees over time, one has to wonder whether this is the path manatees will follow.

Although the results of analyses may not paint a rosy picture, it is good to have scientific data to inform decisions and to provide insights into unperceived dangers to a population. Forewarned is forearmed, as they say. The good news for manatees is that they are not as skewed toward the K-strategist pole as are some other marine mammals, which means that their potential to maintain or increase their populations is better than scientists used to think. The recurring caution that must be remembered is that K is not a constant—the human population in Florida has changed and continues to change the habitat manatees occupy, with both obvious and subtle impacts.

Searching for
the Magic Number

I MENTIONED IN THE previous chapter some models that attempt to provide insight into possible trajectories for manatee populations in Florida. Few topics associated with manatees have generated as much heat (but unfortunately little light!) as the apparently simple questions asked by many individuals and interest groups: How many manatees are there? How many manatees is enough?

The numbers game for manatees has provided considerable frustration for all sides. Part of the problem is the simple scientific truth that it is extremely unlikely that scientists and managers will ever know exactly how many manatees exist. Another part of the problem lies in a misunderstanding of the numbers that exist.

On the surface, it would seem to be a simple task to use either aerial or ground surveys to just count how many manatees exist. However, manatees often occupy turbid water or areas where vegetation hangs over the surface, obscuring the animals. Furthermore, even in clear water, it is possible to miss seeing manatees because of glare on the surface of the water or, if there is much wind, choppiness of the surface.

Scientists like myself have attempted to count manatees when they aggregate in the winter at warm-water refuges such as power plant discharges and natural springs. But the same problems with visibility may exist at these locations, and even when true counts can be obtained directly or from photographs, there remains a nagging uncertainty regarding the number of animals that choose not to seek refuge from the cold and thereby remain uncounted during surveys of the aggregation sites.

Thus counting of manatees has not been as useful as scientists and managers would like. Nonetheless, scientists have gained certain insights from efforts to count manatees using aerial surveys.

One of the more useful approaches to censusing manatees has been winter aerial surveys of Florida Power & Light Company (FPL) plants. Conducted using relatively few surveyors (which reduces the amount of variability in effectiveness of counting by different people) and similar methods from year to year, the surveys have been done every year since 1977. Bruce Craig of Purdue University and other statisticians have applied sophisticated statistics and models to the data. As a result, certain trends in temperature-adjusted counts have suggested general patterns of population change. For example, along the east (Atlantic) coast of Florida, the analyses have suggested that the manatee population grew in size at an annual rate between 6 percent and 8 percent through the late 1980s, but that the population has leveled off, or even started decreasing, since the mid-1990s. Along the southwestern coast of Florida (specifically around the Fort Myers power plant), the aerial survey trend analyses have only been conducted through 1991, and the counts up to that time suggested that the population in that area was stable; however, since that time the manatee subpopulation in southwestern Florida has experienced extremely high watercraft-related mortality as well as a devastating red tide outbreak.[1] Bruce Craig and I are working to update the analyses of the survey data from the area of the Fort Myers power plant.

Other site-specific aerial and ground surveys have occurred at natural warm-water sources such as Crystal River (the site of most of the photographs in this book) and Blue Spring State Park. Although the statistical treatments of the survey data have not been similar to those done for the Florida Power & Light Company plants, it seems clear that more and more animals use such resources during cold winters. At Blue Spring, for example, Ranger Wayne Hartley has documented from the ground around 150 manatees in winter 1999–2000, whereas his predecessors observed no more than 25 there during any winter in the 1970s. Similarly, when Woody Hartman did his landmark study of manatee behavioral ecology at Crystal River in the mid to late 1960s, fewer than 40 animals used the area, but now Ranger Joyce Kleen may spot over 350 manatees when she does an aerial survey on a frosty winter morning.

Other aerial surveys, called *synoptic* (or *same time*) surveys, have been used to attempt to indicate the minimum population of manatees occupying Florida waters. The synoptic surveys were initiated after the state legislature in 1991 mandated an annual census as a means to learn exactly how many manatees exist—this was actually done despite the belief of most scientists that synoptic surveys could never satisfy this goal. The surveys involve a statewide effort to count manatees following passage of one or two winter cold fronts each year. These surveys are plagued by the same deficiencies as are all aerial surveys, but they also lack the observer and survey-route consistency, as well as a reasonable number of replicates, to impart the same statistical power that characterizes the surveys of the Florida Power & Light Company plants. The few synoptic surveys have produced extremely variable counts from year to year, which represent simply "raw counts," uncorrected for temperature or other variables. Hence, modelers and population biologists generally consider the synoptic survey results to be inappropriate for assessing trends, despite the temptation to try to use them in this way.

Nonetheless, the synoptic surveys have provided some interesting insights. Most notably, the surveys provide a window into obtaining an estimate of the minimum number of manatees that occupy Florida's waters. On January 5–6, 2001, the count was an astounding 3,276 manatees, several hundred animals (633, to be exact) higher than the previous high count. This unprecedented count spawned intensive debate about what it means.

As noted above, individuals have been inclined to take the January 2001 count and other synoptic counts, or similar survey results, at face value and have attempted, inappropriately, to use the uncorrected counts to infer trends in the manatee population. Using such an approach, it has seemed an inescapable conclusion that the manatee population continues to grow at a high rate.

Interestingly, the counts around the Florida Power & Light Company plants on January 5, 2001, and January 24, 2001, both exceeded 1,300 manatees, representing about 450 more manatees than were counted during any similar survey over the previous 23 years. It is extremely difficult to understand how there could be such a dramatic increase in the numbers of manatees in 2001, given the slowness of manatee breeding. I believe, with 28 years of aerial surveys under my belt, that the recent high counts do not reflect an increase in population as much as they reflect some other factors.

Aerial survey counts certainly depend on how many manatees are present in a particular location. The number of manatees present at a warm-water refuge, in turn, depends on the intensity and duration of cold weather; following mild or brief cold fronts, only the "wimpy" manatees choose to loll in the warm water, whereas during extremely cold times a great many manatees are motivated to move to the warm-water refuges. But the aerial survey counts depend on other factors as well. For example, the best time to obtain an optimal count in winter, regardless of how many manatees are present, is on a calm day (which minimizes surface chop and turbidity) when the sun shines brightly (thereby inducing manatees to bask at the surface). In January 2001, all of the necessary criteria for extremely high counts of manatees occurred: some of the coldest weather on record for peninsular Florida, and prolonged duration of that cold, followed by several calm, sunny days. In all my years of doing aerial surveys to count manatees, January 2001 produced the best survey conditions I can recall.

After three decades of doing aerial surveys, I recognize imperfections in them, but I am reluctant to take a couple of high counts as indicative of a trend—a minimum population estimate, sure, but not a trend. I am much more comfortable with trend analyses using data from the long-term, oft-repeated surveys of the power plants or of other independent databases that corroborate what the power plant surveys suggest.

Catherine Langtimm, a population biologist with the U.S. Geological Survey, has developed analyses for just such an independent database. As Bruce Craig and I have done with aerial survey data, Langtimm and her colleagues have taken advantage of another long-term database for manatees. It involves a catalog of photographs of manatees that are individually recognizable based on their scar patterns. The catalog contains around 2,000 distinctive individual manatees these days, and it goes back more than 30 years.

The analysis of the photographic database, like that of the power plant surveys, involves sophisticated statistics and models. The analyses provide estimates of year-to-year survival of individually recognizable adult manatees, with a level of credibility, or robustness, not obtainable with even the best analyses of aerial survey data. What the survival estimations tell us is this:

- The manatee subpopulation in northwestern peninsular Florida has an extremely healthy adult survival rate (averaging 95.6 percent and ranging between 94.3 percent and 96.9 percent);[2]

- the manatee subpopulation in the upper St. Johns River (upstream, south of Palatka in northeastern Florida) also has a healthy adult survival rate (averaging 96.0 percent), although it varies more from year to year (ranging from 93.7 percent to 98.2 percent) than is the case for northwestern Florida manatees;

- the subpopulation of manatees along the Atlantic coast of Florida (Georgia border to Miami, including the lower St. Johns River) has a much lower average adult survival rate (93.7 percent), and it varies from 92.1 percent to 95.2 percent in a given year; and

- estimates of adult survival for manatees along the central western and southwestern coasts of Florida (Tampa Bay to Whitewater Bay) are not available as of January 2002, but are expected from scientists at the Florida Marine Research Institute soon. Preliminary analyses have suggested that adult survival there has been comparable to that along the Atlantic coast (and is therefore cause for concern).[3] The data for the southwestern and central western parts of Florida are not as complete as for other parts of the state.

What do such figures for adult survival actually mean in terms of the status of regional subpopulations of manatees? Before answering that question, it is important to clarify that, for K-strategists such as manatees, the most important demographic group for the long-term health and well-being of the population is the adults, and especially the adult females. If the survival of adult females is jeopardized, so is the long-term future of the species, as Marmontel's population viability analysis (mentioned in chapter 3) clarified and quantified.

For manatees, the adult survival estimates have led a group of scientists that constitute the Manatee Population Status Working Group to state that the manatee subpopulations in northeastern Florida and the upper St. Johns River have exhibited sustained growth. However, the adult survival estimates for the Atlantic coast are lower than what would be necessary to sustain population growth. Working group members endorsed the results of Langtimm and her colleagues' work showing that, following a period of growth that lasted through the 1980s, the Atlantic coast population of manatees has stabilized or may be in decline—in other words, almost exactly what the analysis of the winter power plant survey data for the same general region indicated.

Thus two independent long-term databases both suggest that the trend for the Atlantic coast subpopulation of manatees may be cause for concern at present. That concern is exacerbated by the fact that around 47 percent of all Florida manatees belong to that subpopulation, whereas only about 16 percent constitute the two increasing subpopulations in the upper St. Johns River and in northwestern Florida.

Among the three subpopulations for which adult survival estimates exist, the Atlantic coast subpopulation is noteworthy for the extent of human-related mortality of manatees due to collisions with watercraft, entrapment in automatic flood control structures and canal locks, entanglement in fishing gear, and other causes. In southwestern and central western Florida, the second largest manatee subpopulation (consisting of about 37 percent of all the manatees in Florida) also experiences very high human-related mortality (along with eye-catching levels of natural mortality due to cold stress and red tides), and, as noted, preliminary analyses suggest that adult survival of manatees there approximates what it is on the Atlantic coast. And here's the real concern: If manatee numbers are barely (or not even) holding their own in 2002, what will happen when the human population, with all of its attendant activities and impacts, doubles in 30 years—basically a couple of generations of manatees?[4] Without conservative, creative, and proactive planning and a commitment to have better balance, it seems inevitable that as numbers of humans rise, numbers of manatees and of other species can only drop.

The most recent Florida Manatee Recovery Plan based its recommendations on those of the Manatee Population Status Working Group (composed of scientists who specialize in population modeling and in some cases have no vested interest in manatees). The 2001 plan provided the following as benchmarks for healthy manatee populations:

1. that the average annual rate for adult survival equal or exceed 90 percent;

2. that the average annual percentage of adult female manatees accompanied by young (first- or second-year) calves equal or exceed 40 percent; and

3. that the average annual percentage of population growth equal or exceed 0 percent.

In each case, the plan states that the benchmark should be demonstrated statistically within a 95 percent confidence interval. The U.S. Fish and Wildlife Service believes that achieving these benchmarks for each of the four subpopulations for a period of 20 years would provide a measure of confidence regarding the status of manatees that would be sufficient to take the species off the endangered species list, as long as certain other criteria relating to habitat protection were also satisfied.

The criteria originally developed by the Manatee Population Status Working Group were defendable based on their scientific merit, and they favored conservatism with the vulnerable K-strategists. The criteria were not originally going to be adopted by the Fish and Wildlife Service; ultimately, however, the Service did adopt them (albeit in a somewhat weaker form than originally proposed), thereby providing a clearer, more scientifically based assessment than in past iterations of the Florida Manatee Recovery Plan of what constitutes healthy manatee populations. The criteria are also noteworthy and commendable because they are *not* simply based on counts of manatees—a tempting oversimplification for reasons noted below. Rather, the criteria explicitly consider at least some aspects of life history of the manatee population. This level of analysis and examination is extremely important, but all too often managers either lack the data to include meaningful demographic criteria or they simply neglect to do so.

Even without an in-depth understanding of demography and demographic analyses, simply applying common sense can illustrate the importance of having some understanding of age- and sex-related criteria. For example, a population of people that averages 30 years in age, and that has some balance in terms of age structure, has a different likelihood of being able to sustain itself than does a population comprising only retirees—certainly the latter population will have a lower annual adult survival than will the former. As another example, a human (or other) population skewed heavily toward males has a different ability to sustain itself or increase than does one with a balanced sex ratio. These simple examples illustrate the value of developing an understanding of species demographics and of including demographic criteria in recovery plans or other management-oriented documents. This does not mean that the demographic criteria in the latest manatee recovery plan are comprehensive—they're not, but they do represent an important step forward in terms of assessment of manatee status.

The above information on population size and trends among living manatees needs to be considered in the context of information on manatee mortality. In 2001, 325 dead manatees were recovered, easily the second highest number ever recorded in a year. The only time this number was exceeded was in 1996, when 149 manatees died during a red tide event.

In the five-year period between 1996 and 2000, an average of 291 manatees was killed each year, with, on average, 85 (29 percent) of those deaths being due to human causes. For the previous three five-year periods, the comparable figures are shown in table 4.

The percentages reported in table 4 compare five-year averages. Even equating those percentages to annual rates, between the 1991–95 period and the 1996–2000 period, for example, human-related mortality alone rose by an average of over 9 percent a year. Compare this value with the best-case scenario for population growth provided by Marsh's calculations noted earlier in this chapter: 6.6 percent per year under optimal conditions. Does this seem like a realistic or ideal formula for long-term population sustainability?

Overall, if one considers the five-year averaged increments in table 4, for the 20-year period between 1981 and 2000, manatee mortality increased by 177 animals (an increase of 155 percent) and human-related manatee mortality increased by 53 animals (an increase of 166 percent). That's a lot—especially for an endangered species that is receiving considerable special protection provided by several state and federal laws. Even my extremely simplistic analyses shown here demonstrate that factors that kill manatees are not under control, despite ongoing efforts and admirable intentions.

To at least some extent, the higher levels of mortality should be attributed to the documented increasing population size of manatees through the 1980s and early 1990s, as discussed above. What is quite worrisome is that the trend for increased total and human-related mortality of manatees continues, even

Table 4. Comparison of total and human-related mortality of manatees.

Period	Average total mortality/year[a] and percentage increase over previous 5-year average	Average human-related mortality/year[b] and percentage increase over previous 5-year average
1981–1985	114	32
1986–1990	153 (34%)	51 (59%)
1991–1995	177 (16%)	58 (14%)
1996–2000	291 (64%)	85 (47%)
2001	325 (12%)	88 (2%)

[a] Total mortality includes deaths due to a variety of natural factors (for example, red tides, disease, cold weather), human factors (for example, watercraft collisions, crushing/drowning in canal locks or flood gates, ingestion of hooks or debris, and entanglement in fishing gear), and undetermined causes. The category of "perinatal" mortality refers to very young (near birth) manatees for which cause of death cannot be determined; it is quite likely that some perinatal deaths are due to human factors (for example, a mother manatee being killed or injured and abandoning her calf).

[b] Human-related mortality includes watercraft collisions, crushing/drowning in canal locks and flood gates, ingestion of debris, entanglement, shooting, or other causes where there is *certainty* that humans caused the death of a manatee. Although perinatal mortality *is probably* related to human activities in some cases, perinatal deaths are not considered as human-related.

though the population trends suggest that the largest subpopulation of manatees (along the Atlantic coast) is no longer increasing in size. It raises the question: Have we reached the point where, even with some effective conservation measures in place, the multiple direct and indirect impacts of the human population on manatees cannot be sustained? Stated otherwise, in terms of maintenance of living resources for Florida, have we reached carrying capacity for levels of human population and human activities in the state? There are several variables at work here, including but not limited to: human population size in Florida, slated to double over the next three decades; manatee population size, which may not be sustainable in the face of further human population increases; and the behavior of the humans, which *can either exacer-*

bate or mitigate (depending on will) the effects of more and more people. It seems clear that all three factors—twice as many people, the same number of manatees (and indeed of other living resources), and human behaviors similar to those of today—cannot coexist into the future. So difficult choices are faced by people in Florida, among other places.

A couple of points of clarification may be useful. The scientists working at the State's Marine Mammal Pathobiology Laboratory are extremely good at what they do, not just according to me but also according to eminent pathologists, anatomists, and veterinarians who reviewed that program's operations in 2000. However, the state of the art for marine mammal necropsies is not sufficiently advanced in any facility to routinely allow the diagnosis of some subtle effects of human activities on manatees, and year after year about one-third of all manatee deaths occur for reasons that cannot be determined because: (1) a carcass is simply too decomposed to allow a cause of death to be determined, or (2) the cause of death is elusive, given the analyses that are either possible technologically or are actually done. For example, funds are not available to permit a full range of toxicological analyses to be done on tissues from dead manatees; but it is likely that certain toxic metals, such as butyltins, that have been used in marine paints to retard growth of organisms on boat bottoms and that are sequestered in sediments where manatees forage, may be ingested by manatees and lead to impaired health and diminished survival. We just don't know. We also do not know the extent to which escalating perinatal deaths may have human causes. But we do know that the documented levels of human-caused manatee mortality represent just the *minimum levels*—they only reveal human-caused mortality that scientists have been able to ascertain, and as new laboratory techniques improve the resolution of analyses, or as funds permit additional analyses, we are likely to find the number and percentage of human-related manatee deaths increasing to an even greater extent than has occurred to date.

This leads to another important clarification: the effects of sublethal injuries or other problems that debilitate manatees. When marine mammal scientists assess the status of a population or species, the process generally involves an attempt to quantify how many animals exist and how many die each year. These sorts of data are important to have, but they certainly do not tell the whole story.

To illustrate this point, consider the long-term prospects for two different groups of 3,500 people (about the same number as the highest count of manatees). The first group comprises 3,500 college students strolling around a campus—a group of young, healthy people in the prime of life. The potential for them to live a long time and produce offspring is high, making the long-term prospects excellent. Now consider a group of 3,500 young AIDS patients confined to hospital beds; although they are in the same age class as the college students, their long-term prospects don't look so rosy. Numbers alone don't tell the whole story about the status of a group.

Tom O'Shea and his colleagues recently wrote about the effects of sublethal watercraft collisions with manatees.[5] Imagine the pain that a cut several inches into the muscles of the back, and even into the lungs, must cause. Further imagine, as several scientists have suggested or documented, the impairment of reproduction that occurs as a result of the injury, ranging from possible abandonment of a calf to cessation of normal hormone cycling leading to an inability to conceive. Consider that chronically seriously injured manatees may suffer from depressed immune systems, making them vulnerable to infections, toxins and toxicants, and other agents. Note that severely injured manatees may have trouble migrating, feeding, or doing other normal behaviors. Finally, recall from chapter 1 that manatees may be struck as many as 50 different times in their life-spans, and multiply all the problems noted above by an order of magnitude. To date, there has been relatively little documentation of the effects of acute or chronic physical debilitation on important aspects of manatee biology, such as reproductive performance or potential, but what has been documented leads to an inescapable conclusion that injured animals cannot behave and breed optimally.

In addition to the complications and debilitations that occur due to watercraft collisions, manatees exposed to severe or prolonged cold weather or to intense red tide outbreaks may suffer from decreased competence of the immune system, with some of the same unwanted effects that occur following severe injuries. There appear to be extremely subtle effects of environmental (and some anthropogenic) problems on manatees.

I have already noted that Butch Rommel and I find it hard to believe that manatees are able to survive even moderately cold weather in Florida, and that the answer, we think, lies in the enormity of the large intestine, where countless microbes break down the cellulose that constitutes much of the manatee diet and thus produce heat. We plan to assess the extent of such heat production in manatees fed different diets, but we already have some questions that we wonder about:

- When manatees travel to and remain near warm-water refuges in winter, does lack of food near certain refuges mean that the "internal furnace" of manatees shuts down? Does this compromise their survival when they disperse into cold water?

- Is the reason manatees in Florida are more rotund than manatees of the same species in South and Central America related simply to Florida manatees' acquiring, through natural selection, a larger furnace (large intestine) to keep warm?

- What happens to the gut microbes if a manatee consumes oil-coated vegetation following an oil spill? Do the microbes die, leaving the manatee with no way to break down cellulose to acquire nutrients and heat? Similarly, what happens to the microbes if a manatee consumes a lot of brevetoxin during a red tide bloom?

Little things (pun intended) can make a huge difference in the health and well-being of individual manatees, and ultimately in their ability to reproduce and maintain a healthy population. Yet to date scientists have little information regarding what constitutes a healthy individual manatee or manatee population. And because the focus of management has been on the more blatant factors that kill manatees, reaching an adequate understanding of the subtleties has not been adequately championed.

Among the subtleties are the effects of toxicants on manatees (or on most species, for that matter). I noted above that an oil spill could cause acute problems for manatees that ingest residues and inadvertently destroy their gut microbe population. However, what about the effects of chronic low levels of oil, or of metals, chlorinated hydrocarbons, and other chemical pollutants? Although high levels of copper have been noted in manatee tissues, the effects of high copper can only be speculated at this point. Levels of other toxicants in manatee tissues have not been especially high, *but* scientists have really only looked at a small subset of the possible toxicants. The relative lack of high levels of toxicants in manatee tissues does raise the question, though: Why *don't* manatees accumulate high levels of some chemical pollutants in their bodies as dolphins and many other marine mammals do? The answer has to do, at least in part, with the position manatees occupy in the food web (that is, their trophic level). Species that exist at a lower trophic level, such as the herbivores, tend not to bioaccumulate some types of toxicants as much as do animals at higher trophic levels (namely carnivores). Thus, even though manatees live for many years and might be considered as prime candidates to accumulate high levels of toxicants over the years, their herbivorous diet provides some protection from that problem for chemicals such as pesticides and mercury.

It should be borne in mind, though, that it is awfully tough to know what a certain part per billion of a toxicant in a tissue means in terms of animal health. To be sure, when toxicologists find very high levels of a chemical pollutant in the tissues of individuals of a particular species, it raises a red flag that problems may exist. However, tissue levels tell a distressingly small part of the story because different species, and even individuals within a species, have different innate abilities to detoxify chemicals that enter their bodies. In other words, levels of a toxicant that may be lethal to one species may have no noticeable effect on another. Similarly, the presence of certain toxicant levels in tissues can have sublethal consequences; imagine if a toxicant such as copper did not kill a manatee, but rather made it sluggish and less responsive than usual. Such an animal might be a prime candidate to be struck by a boat and killed.

Some of the unexamined toxicants may be of particular interest. The butyltins, for example, have been used in boat-bottom paints to reduce fouling. The butyltins are extremely toxic to many other species, and in a species like the manatee, which lives for decades, could build to dangerous levels. Other toxicants also merit some investigation in terms of their levels in manatee tissues.

Although it is not politically, ethically, or legally acceptable to dose manatees with toxicants to assess effects on the animals' health or reproductive performance, it would be very useful to examine tissue levels of suites of toxicants and anatomical or clinical signs that health is being impaired in some way. This sort of work has been done, but could usefully be expanded.

Another fruitful area of research should involve examining the cellular and molecular mechanisms that manatees use to bind or detoxify particular toxic chemicals that enter their bodies. This relatively new approach to research has already been applied to other marine mammals and could provide important insights for manatees as well.

A major "black hole" exists in terms of establishing habitat-related criteria for downlisting or delisting manatees from the U.S. Endangered Species List. I remarked earlier in this chapter about the formation and recommendations of a Manatee Population Status Working Group to advise the Recovery Team and inform decisions about appropriate population criteria that need to be achieved to demonstrate that Florida manatees are out of danger. There has been a recommendation for many years that the U.S. Fish and Wildlife Service form a parallel entity, the Habitat Working Group, comprising scientists and other stakeholders whose charge will include listing habitat criteria that need to be met for managers to be assured that manatees are in good shape. That group met for the first time in February 2002, and a subgroup called the Warm Water Task Force (charged with reviewing and making recommendations regarding research or management actions relating to manatees' warm-water needs in winter) has met on several occasions.

It must be recognized that the habitat needs of a healthy manatee population are not known with any great resolution. People acknowledge that manatees need access to warm water in winter, but how warm, for how long? People know manatees need aquatic vegetation to eat, but how much and of what quality? People have suggested that manatees need quiet areas to calve, but where and when? People know that noise and chemical pollution are likely to affect manatee behavior and health, but which chemicals, at what concentrations, are unacceptably bad, and how much noise, at what frequencies, constitutes a problem?

It may be surprising to note that, for particular species, not all human-related changes are negative. That has absolutely been the case for manatees. Dredge and fill work has not been generally recognized as an environmental boon in Florida, but coupled with the introduction of exotic aquatic weeds such as hydrilla and water hyacinth (again, not a good thing environmentally), the activity has promoted the growth of more manatee food than probably existed in certain locations in the past. Similarly, one can argue that the production of thermal discharges by power plants has led to certain environmental problems, but those same discharges have allowed manatees to expand their winter range in some parts of the state and presumably have been a factor in the growth of regional subpopulations of manatees.

The reality is that habitat quality in Florida is not assured in 2002. It will be even less assured in 2030, when there will be twice as many people in the state. Managers would have to make a number of assumptions, some quite nonconservative, if they were to suggest that we either know what the habitat needs of Florida manatees are or that we have safeguarded those needs. And for a K-strategist, poor assumptions that promote loss of habitat can spell the end decisively. We need much better data regarding the needs of manatees and other species, followed or accompanied by proactive, effective policy, before we can feel comfortable.

The point is that counting heads in the field or bodies in the pathobiology laboratory tells an incomplete story. The numbers game can only provide so many insights. The health and well-being of manatees must be factored into acceptable criteria that describe what constitutes an optimal manatee population in Florida.

It seems extremely premature to conjecture about the long-term health and prospects of manatees in Florida. I believe, however, in my gut that the Florida manatee has shown some very clear signs of being in better shape than it was 30 years ago. *If* the population criteria developed in the 2001 Manatee Recovery Plan were met, and *if* I were able to be convinced that habitat in Florida's coastal environments was appropriately safeguarded for the future, I would number myself among the people who strongly support the downlisting (*not* delisting) of manatees to "threatened." Those *ifs* may seem a little daunting and insurmountable, but I don't believe they are impossible to achieve if there is the will to do so. The fact that we may be able to even consider such a change in the status of manatees in the future is a positive reflection on the citizens of Florida, on resource managers, and on the pluckiness and tenacity of manatees.

"Misbehaving" Manatees in Harm's Way

IT HAS BEEN OPINED that manatees must be pretty dumb to keep getting hit by motorboats. I don't think that lack of intelligence is the real problem.

Heaven knows, I am not trying to suggest that manatees would be good contestants on *Jeopardy!* Let's be honest: people have trouble defining what intelligence is in other people. There are over 100 different intelligence quotient (IQ) tests designed to assess how smart our own species is. I think it is a little ambitious (not to mention downright unrealistic) to suggest that we can define or quantify the level of intelligence in other species.

I know that a lot has been made of the communicative and cognitive abilities of some of the "intelligent" nonhuman species such as bottlenose dolphins and chimpanzees. If one compares the brain size and complexity of manatees, as well as the cognitive and other "intellectual" capabilities of manatees, to those of dolphins and chimpanzees, well . . . let's be politically correct and just say that manatees are not quite as cerebral. Although many species of large mammals have rather large brains (the size of the brain and of most other organs is related in a rather predictable relationship to body size), scientists Tom O'Shea and Roger Reep found that manatee brains start out small at birth and grow very slowly, relative to body mass, as they mature. These scientists suggested that (1) the low metabolic rate of manatees may place constraints on growth of a fetal manatee's brain (nervous tissue like the brain is metabolically extremely "expensive" to maintain), and/or (2) the selection for large body size of manatees as they mature (for example, as an adaptation to help stay warm) has caused the usual relationship between brain and body size to erode.

Having said that, I must quickly add that lack of a big brain has absolutely nothing to do with a species' intrinsic value and in no way should diminish the extent to which that species merits conservation. All too often, people tend to value most those species that possess features we admire in ourselves. Slowly but surely a conservation ethic has been developing that reinforces the value of species that have had the gross misfortune to evolve attributes that are only remotely human-like! There will be more on that topic in chapter 7.

For now, the point is that manatees may not be intellectual giants, but they are quite bright enough to have survived in a changing world far longer than our own species has. Manatees, in fact, developed adaptations—morphological, behavioral, and otherwise—that allowed them to occupy an important and specialized niche.

Unfortunately for manatees, the environmental conditions that helped evolutionarily to shape their multiple and diverse adaptations have changed dramatically. What once was adaptive may be less so, or may even be maladaptive in a world shaped so significantly by human activities.

Fully recognizing my earlier admonition that truly natural environments may simply not exist, let us nonetheless consider the world that helped to shape Florida manatees and how that world may be different today. Having done that, let's consider why manatees may be "misbehaving" relative to what they "should" do to survive better in the changing world of the twenty-first century.

Scientists do not have a clear idea of how manatees perceive their world; beyond that, of the many and diverse stimuli that bombard manatees (or any organism for that matter), scientists do not know exactly which ones are really meaningful. However, there are some interesting studies and observations that shed light on how manatees perceive and react to their world.

For example, the world is filled with scents and tastes (chemicals) that can convey meaningful information to the recipient. For humans, the senses of smell (olfaction) and taste (gustation) are not as important as is the sense of vision, but even for people, chemical cues in the air or in what we eat and drink make a difference in our behavior: "Let's hurry, I smell cookies that Mom made"; "Watch out for spilled bleach"; "Be careful, I smell smoke from a fire nearby"; "I hate liver." People are aware that species such as salmon use chemicals dissolved in river water to locate their natal streams, to which they return to spawn. In fact, it seems quite likely from behavioral observations that chemical cues mean a great deal to manatees—chemical cues may even be among the most important social and environmental stimuli for manatees.

Manatees mouth one another frequently, and they return to favorite rubbing posts, which they also mouth. This behavior suggests that manatees may learn something about the identity or status of other manatees by taste. It has long been suspected, for example, that male manatees may use their chemical sensitivity to determine the breeding status of female manatees and to locate females in estrus. Perhaps reproductive success of manatees is linked closely with their ability to detect particular compounds such as estrogen in water.

In addition, manatees may navigate and orient themselves using chemicals that are unrelated to social or sexual cues. The animals show great ability to locate freshwater sources, and intrepid scientists even use cleverly designed traps (namely a running hose suspended over a shallow canal) to lure manatees to a spot where they can be easily captured for study. In an interesting experiment, scientists recently showed that harbor seals (*Phoca vitulina,* another coastal marine mammal but unrelated to manatees) are able to detect a faint freshwater plume and follow it to its source. My colleague Gordon Bauer of New College and I hypothesize that manatees may have at least as great a sensitivity to fresh water as do the harbor seals, and we hope to work with colleagues and manatees at Disney's Living Seas to attempt to clarify that hypothesis. In addition to finding fresh water, manatees, like salmon, may use chemical cues to enhance their ability to locate and return to the same feeding, breeding, or other biologically important sites every year. In light of all the wastes, toxicants, runoff, bilge-water, and other "stuff" people dump into coastal waterways, it makes sense, I think, to raise the question: What would happen to manatees (or other wildlife species that depend on chemical cues to navigate) if they were unable to return successfully to sites that they require, due to people's inadvertently changing the chemical nature of coastal waters in ways that mask or change the special chemical cues on which the animals rely to orient and navigate?

Manatees may also use their ability to detect certain chemicals to avoid eating plants that could possibly cause problems. John Bengtson, for example, studied manatee food preferences and found that the animals avoided certain species of plant known to contain noxious chemicals. Other studies have confirmed that blue-green algae, which contain toxins, tend to be avoided.

Manatees, naturally, would need to possess the means to detect such chemicals. People have special areas of sensory cells within our nasal cavities, as well as taste buds on our tongues. Manatees, not surprisingly, keep their valve-like nostrils closed when they are underwater, but sometimes they appear to sniff the air when they breathe. Biologists do not know if they have sensory cells in their noses, and the bones that underlie areas where such cells exist in many other species (the cribriform plates) are small in manatees. Sensory biologists Douglas Wartzok and Darlene Ketten have described the manatee olfactory system as "very rudimentary."[1]

The potential for manatees to taste is a bit clearer, since taste buds are located at the back of their tongues; however, the number of taste buds in manatees is lower than in many herbivorous terrestrial mammals. The nature of what manatees can taste and their sensitivity to particular tastes remain murky. Finally, in some animals for which detection of chemical cues is extremely important (for example, vultures) there is a special structure, called a *vomeronasal organ,* associated with the roof of the mouth. The vomeronasal organ imparts enhanced ability to detect particular chemicals. Manatees lack this special organ.

Although manatees appear to use chemical cues for a variety of important reasons, as in humans and other complex species there is actually a suite of sensory information that, when perceived and processed, sometimes leads to a particular response. In humans, vision predominates, and in manatees visual cues are also important, but less so than in ourselves.

Field biologists have long conjectured that manatees use vision when inspecting an approaching diver or canoe, as well as other objects. On the other hand, older anatomical literature describing the manatee eye and its potential to see well suggested that the species has abysmal vision.

More recent studies have been illuminating, although the species seems to have imposed some of its usual paradoxical attributes on its visual system. Manatees, as it turns out, have both rods and cones in their retinas, although rods (which are most useful during times when light is dim) predominate. The presence of cones suggests that manatees may have at least moderately good visual acuity, meaning that they can see objects distinctly. In addition, manatees possess the ability to see some colors, thanks to their cones.

The manatee eye seems to be best adapted for conditions of relatively low light. However, unlike the eye of a cat or other animal that is adapted to functioning well during low-light conditions, manatees lack a *tapetum lucidum,* a layer of crystals located behind the retina that causes "eye-shine" and functions to enhance vision when light is limited.

At least a couple of other cues may provide important information to manatees: those cues are detected by the senses of touch (tactile sensation) and hearing (acoustics). Sirenians have extremely well developed sensory hairs on their faces and bodies. Bristles on the face of a manatee are used with great sensitivity to explore the environment (food, ropes, obstacles) and other manatees. The bristles are quite unusual, however, in that they can be everted to help grasp and manipulate food and other objects.

The hairs located on the body of a manatee are connected to nerves. Almost 30 years ago, I postulated that these hairs might serve something of the same function as the lateral line of fishes, namely to sense currents and pressure waves around the animal. In cases where such currents are produced by nearby manatees, the stimuli might help animals to coordinate and synchronize their behaviors, such as surfacing to breathe, when in murky waters. Recently neuroanatomist Roger Reep has provided evidence that manatee hairs may do precisely this.

I have saved a discussion of manatee acoustics for last for two reasons: it is the sensory topic about which scientists currently know the most, and it is the focus of considerable controversy. So what do scientists say about manatee hearing?

There have been several studies that have employed different methods to assess this capability. One study played various sounds to Florida manatees and determined which ones produced nerve impulses (what are technically called *auditory evoked potentials*) indicative of the nerves associated with the ear's being stimulated. That study suggested that manatees are most sensitive to sounds with frequencies around 1.5 kilohertz—roughly the frequency of sound that a television emergency warning signal tone makes. Another study carefully considered the anatomy of the manatee ear and suggested that the frequencies that manatees should hear best would be slightly higher, namely around 5 kilohertz (similar to a smoke detector signal). Studies of Amazonian manatees—not Florida manatees—using auditory evoked potentials found that this species hears best those sounds that are between 5 and 20 kilohertz. This same range of solid hearing capabilities was also found (but with optimal hearing occurring with frequencies around 16 kilohertz—about as high-pitched a signal as the human ear can detect) during studies of Florida manatees that played sounds to two trained, captive manatees and used the behavior of the animals to tell the scientists what they had heard (a technique that produces so-called *behavioral audiograms*). The latter study provided some evidence that manatees hear sounds with frequencies as high as 46 kilohertz. It bears mentioning that manatees produce sounds (squeaks and squeals) that range in frequency from about 1 kilohertz to about 16 kilohertz—not surprisingly, this is basically the same frequency range that scientists believe they hear best.

Before turning to what these data mean—or may mean—there is one more factor to consider: manatees' ability to localize sound underwater, that is, to tell the direction from which a sound comes. As anyone who has done much swimming or diving can attest, humans lack this ability when their heads are submerged. Dolphins and other cetaceans, however, can do so, thanks in part to a fat body located in each side of the lower jaw that "traps" sound and channels it to each ear. Manatees lack such a fat-filled lower jaw, but part of their "cheekbone" (technically called a *zygomatic process*) is porous and filled with oil that contains many of the lipid components of the lower jaw fat of dolphins. Since each cheekbone abuts the ear on that side of the head, it is possible (not proven!) that the cheekbone is the conduit for sound to the manatee ear and that it provides some ability to help localize certain sounds.

Studies of hearing in manatees have great practical importance. As has been noted earlier, manatees are often struck and killed or severely injured by watercraft in Florida. Like many other Floridians, I love to boat and I do so a lot in my work; crawling along at a very slow speed isn't something I especially relish. But like many other Floridians I would hate to have my vessel hurt or kill anything. And like many other Floridians, I once wondered: Do the manatees simply not hear the boats?

The implications of the question are *not trivial*! Answers will impact peoples' livelihoods, their recreational pleasures, and their quality of life. The answers also impact survival of manatees.

One group of scientists headed by Ed Gerstein and Joe Blue did the behavioral audiogram noted above; they have suggested that manatees may not, in fact, hear boats particularly well, and that the problem is especially evident for slow-moving boats, which produce lower frequencies of sound than do faster boats. If this is true, then it would follow that management efforts to reduce watercraft-related manatee mortality are completely inappropriate, since those efforts have focused on slowing boats down in areas where collisions with manatees have occurred in the past or are likely due to the presence of lots of manatees.

The slowing of the boats as a management tool has been done under the following premises: (1) that this slowing would give boaters more time to detect and avoid manatees; (2) if a collision does occur, presumably the manatee will suffer less severe injury from the impact; (3) that manatees can perceive boats and the direction from which they are coming; and (4) that the slowing of boats provides manatees more time to detect and avoid oncoming vessels. For example, a boat traveling at 30 knots travels about 50 feet per second; thus, if a boat were traveling this fast and the driver observed a manatee 50 feet ahead, there would be an impossibly short amount of time (just one second) in which to react by changing the heading of the boat enough to miss the manatee. Using the same logic for a boat traveling at 5 knots (8 feet per second), the driver would have about 6 seconds to avoid the manatee if the animal were initially spotted 50 feet ahead. Slowing boats down uses the same logic that people use successfully when they establish 15-mile-per-hour speed limits to protect children in school zones.

Well, if manatees do not hear boats well, then it places the entire burden (and according to some an unfair one) of collision avoidance on the boater. But, if manatees can hear faster boats, then, it has been argued, we should do one or both of two things: (1) speed up boat traffic, and/or (2) equip boats with alarm signals that manatees hear better than they do the boats themselves.

There are a lot of issues here: First, there are observations and videos of manatees in the presence of fast- and slow-moving boats demonstrating that the manatees do react, at least under certain circumstances, to the approaching watercraft. Some well-controlled field observations of tagged manatees in areas with few boats indicate that manatees may actually detect boats (even slow-moving ones) under some conditions at ranges of several hundred meters. To be sure, manatees that are engrossed in feeding on dense sea-grasses may miss the signal either due to preoccupation or to the fact that the seagrasses, of their own nature and because they occur in shallow water, may not permit sounds to be propagated well. But biologists who have spent time in the field observing manatees generally feel that manatees can, in fact, perceive boats adequately.

Of even greater concern is the most frequent response of manatees when they hear a boat: the animals flee to deep water, sometimes directly into the path of the boat as it cruises along a channel. Especially if the boat is proceeding quickly, this reaction is a recipe for a collision. Yet it seems to be an instinctive knee-jerk (despite lack of manatee knees) response by the animals to perceived threats; the response and its current apparent maladaptiveness have led me to wonder whether manatees in the past were subjected to predation from terrestrial animals (such as panthers, bears) and Paleo-Indians to the extent that the reflexive action to dive made sense as an adaptive strategy.

Let's say that there is a collision. What then? Let's use a commonsense approach to try to evaluate the consequences: If you are struck by an automobile traveling at 60 miles per hour, you will be badly injured or killed. If you are struck by the same automobile traveling at 3 miles per hour, you will likely survive the initial impact unscathed and even be able to dodge around the oncoming vehicle. The same physics and logic apply to collisions between manatees and boats. All other things being equal, speed kills and causes serious injuries.

But things are not always equal. Size of boats also varies. So let's, once again, adopt a commonsense approach to guessing what factors cause the most damage. Let's say you are struck by a car traveling 20 miles per hour.

The damage could be considerable. However, let's say you are struck by a cocker spaniel traveling at the same speed; you'll probably be just fine. All things being equal, boat size also matters in terms of the extent of injury.

Actually there are data that support the latter idea. Tom Pitchford and his colleagues at the State of Florida's Marine Mammal Pathobiology Laboratory have worked with human forensic specialists and engineers who worked for powerboat manufacturers to carefully analyze the cuts found on deceased manatees. The scientists have shown that, in cases where manatees die because of propeller-inflicted cuts rather than because of "blunt trauma" associated with the impact of a boat, the spacing and other aspects of the cuts indicate that larger boats are generally the culprits.

So although the behavioral audiogram using a couple of captive manatees was carefully done and has suggested that manatee hearing of boats may be an issue, and even though some people have used this suggestion to speculate that slowing of boats may only exacerbate the extent to which manatees are struck and killed by watercraft, work with manatees in the field shows that manatees can hear boats under many circumstances, and the laws of physics suggest that larger boats, with larger propellers, may be responsible for more deaths and serious injuries due to propeller cuts than smaller boats. One should not lose sight of the fact, however, that about *half* of all watercraft-related manatee mortality is due to blunt trauma associated simply with the impact of the collision, not due to cutting. For this reason, the oft-suggested use of propeller guards has not received great support; after all, mandatory propeller guards would only solve part of the problem.

Even a small object can cause a lot of damage when it travels at high speed. Just think about a bullet or arrow. So the blunt trauma injuries and fatalities can occur as a result of strikes by boats of almost any size, if speed is great enough.

Thus, although manatees generally seem to hear boats sufficiently well, this doesn't necessarily provide resolution of all the issues. There are still questions to be answered:

- Would use of alarms on boats increase the distance at which manatees hear boats and permit the animals to get out of harm's way more effectively?

- If so, does it make sense to project even more human-related noise into an already noisy coastal environment?

- Are there other issues associated with boat use in Florida that merit discussion?

- On which party—manatee or human—should the responsibility for avoiding collisions lie? Maritime law suggests the latter.

- Why don't manatees simply learn to get out of the way after they have been struck several times?

- Do manatees habituate to persistent underwater sounds and simply fail to react as they otherwise might?

To address these questions one by one, let me offer the following points of view and opinions. To start, the "right" answer often depends on individual perspectives and values. I simply offer mine as something to consider.

There is concern that manatees will not necessarily react to the alarm sounds in a way that solves the problem. For one thing, until a manatee has ignored the alarm and gotten struck one or more times, it isn't likely to recognize the alarm as a danger sign and take steps to avoid the oncoming boat. This would presumably become a conditioned response that would occur only after at least one negative experience. In addition, if the manatee reacted, it presumably would still respond by hastily seeking a channel—in other words it would go someplace where it placed itself in harm's way. So the jury is out regarding whether an alarm would work anyway. Finally, if hundreds of thousands of boats had the alarms, I can imagine that manatees might habituate to the sound.

Second, there are a lot of marine and aquatic creatures that use sound to communicate to their young, locate predators, locate mates, and otherwise do the things necessary to live and proliferate. The sound levels produced by the natural inhabitants of coastal ecosystems can be quite loud—yet they get overwhelmed at times by the sounds associated with aircraft, boats, drilling, dredge and fill, automobiles traversing bridges, and other sounds produced by people. In some cases, anthropogenic sounds have been so loud that some scientists have suggested they caused whale ear bones to shatter! At a more subtle level of impact, noise pollution has caused marine mammals to avoid important habitat, expend more energy to survive, and alter their migratory routes. One has to wonder—at the ecosystem level—whether it makes sense to project yet more sound from the nearly 900,000 registered boats in Florida. Even if it reduces manatee mortality, is it causing population-level problems for acoustically active fishes (including commercially and recreationally valuable species such as redfish and croakers), dolphins, and many invertebrates?

So the alarms may make some sense at one level, but may not be the best answer overall. That remains to be seen. More generically, the question of possible technological innovations is open for discussion. The State of Florida, in fact, has allocated money to examine whether creative, high-tech approaches might contribute to mitigating the problem of collisions between manatees and watercraft. In 2002, several options are being investigated, including four that use software (for example, voice recognition software) attuned to manatee vocalizations and other sounds to detect such noises, send a signal to a surface beacon, and thereby alert boaters of the presence of manatees nearby. Such approaches, it should be noted, may not always work either (sometimes manatees are silent), but at least they place the burden for mitigating the problem on the boaters rather than on the manatees (except that manatees are obliged to make noise!).

And this brings me to the next question: Are manatees and manatee collisions the only issue here? Some members of the media and others have sometimes painted it so, but this is simply an unacceptable misrepresentation and oversimplification of the situation.

A problematic but all-too-rarely mentioned issue associated with boating in Florida is *human* mortality and serious injury associated with boating accidents. Even though Florida is not the state with the largest number of registered boats (in 2000, for example, Michigan led the way with 1,000,049 registered boats, California followed with 904,863, and Florida came in third with 840,684) it routinely *is* the state with the most human fatalities associated with boating accidents. In 2001, that number was 54, almost as high as the number of manatee deaths (82) from the same cause. The state with the next highest number of human fatalities associated with boating accidents in 2001 was California, with 15 percent fewer deaths (46) than Florida.

Florida also is notorious for its rate of human fatalities. In 2000, the national average was 5.5 human deaths per 1,000 registered boats; Florida, in 2000, was at the national average, *but* the year 2000 represented a somewhat anomalous year—the first time in a decade and a half that Florida did *not* have the largest number of human fatalities due to boating accidents in the United States. In most years, Florida's rate of human fatalities per 1,000 registered boats stands clearly, and sadly, above the national average.

To reinforce a couple of other points, Florida boaters experienced 1,194 reported accidents in 2000: 46 were fatal and 644 involved injuries sufficiently serious to require medical care in excess of first aid. Alcohol was involved in 35 percent of the fatal boating accidents in Florida in 2000, and

Florida ranked second in the nation in terms of alcohol-related boating accidents, placing behind only Missouri in this category. Finally, in terms of an age breakdown of the fatal accidents in Florida in 2000, 37 percent involved boat drivers who were 52 years old or older, whereas only 16 percent involved drivers who were 21 years old or younger.

Licenses and boater education are not required for most of Florida's boaters. Thus, many boaters operate their vessels absent a great deal of knowledge or experience.

I asked the question: Are there other issues? I think the answer is yes—we should be working to create safer conditions for humans on the waterways of Florida, not just for manatees. And if the deaths and injuries of people and manatees aren't compelling enough reasons to reconsider what occurs on Florida's waterways, how about the millions of dollars that boating accidents cost each year (about $7 million just in property damage in 2000, to say nothing of health costs and insurance claims)? Despite their seriousness, the broad implications regarding this important topic rarely arise in the press; the general public apparently perceives, or has been led to perceive, that the whole controversy about boats in Florida centers around manatees.

Surprisingly to some people, other large marine vertebrates of concern to the public also are struck and killed by boats. Bottlenose dolphins, agile, quick, and perceptive as they are, still get struck and injured or killed by boats on occasion. So do sea turtles. This seems to occur especially when lots of speeding boats occupy an area, as occurs during races.

People who enjoy fishing and other waterborne activities should note another potential effect of boats. Studies have demonstrated that a lot of high-speed boating increases turbidity, thereby limiting seagrass productivity. This, in turn, will limit shellfish productivity, fish productivity, bird productivity, dolphin productivity . . . you get the idea. And reduced fish and shellfish populations (among others) will hit commercial fishermen in their pocketbooks and will diminish the pleasures of recreational anglers as well. Reduced dolphin and bird populations will hurt certain types of tourism—another economic hit. Again . . . you get the idea. We collectively should attempt to ensure that neither boating nor other human activities reduce the health and extent of the natural resources that a wide range of human stakeholders enjoy and use so much in Florida.

So let's return to the idea that alarms *may* have a chance of reducing (not eliminating) manatee mortality. The alarms *may not* be good for the environment, and the alarms will certainly *not* prevent human fatalities due to boat accidents, turbidity, and reduced productivity (with its attendant economic problems). And a reliance on alarms *may* even cause some boaters to be less careful and alert. If alarms are only a partial fix that carries certain downsides, are they an answer that we should pursue aggressively? And if they are only a partial fix of the issues of 2002, do they have any hope of being the fix when our population doubles, the number of boats doubles, and overall impacts double 30 years from now?

I also wonder whether the answer should shift the burden of avoidance to manatees. Humans introduce more and more chemicals, noise, physical disturbances, and other factors into coastal ecosystems. Manatees in some parts of their range already exhibit clear behavioral changes associated with human activities—these changes include apparently increasing levels of nocturnal behavior, presumably to avoid increasing levels of hunting, noise, and disturbance associated with people. Is it the responsibility of the natural residents of the world to learn to either avoid us and our artifacts or perish? The emerging belief that humans should be stewards argues against this perspective. Domning's essay "Why Save the Manatee?" provides some interesting points on this topic—and places the burden on the appropriate party, in my opinion: the humans.

I finally arrive at my last question: Why do manatees get hit so much? Picture yourself in the parking lot of a busy shopping mall at Christmas. Cars are moving at different speeds and from different directions as you try to walk across the parking lot. Without extremely close attention, you might step in front of an oncoming vehicle, and sometimes it gets a little confusing as to which car poses the greatest threat.

Now imagine that you periodically are required to step in front of the vehicle of your choice. If you misjudge its speed, or if you focus too much on that vehicle and not on others, you'll get hit.

That's what happens, I think, to manatees sometimes. Like the pedestrian above, manatees have to traverse areas of busy, multidirectional traffic. Since they must breathe every couple of minutes, they are required to surface and become vulnerable to being struck. If they miscalculate which of the many vessels is closest or fastest when they approach the surface to fill their lungs . . . well, you get the idea.

I think that confusion under the surface of our busy waterways contributes to the problem. So does the innate tendency of frightened manatees to seek a channel, which unfortunately places them in harm's way. All too often they don't get another chance.

State and federal managers have attempted to give the manatees the best chance both of avoiding a collision in the first place (by reducing boat speed in critical locations, limiting boat access in areas where problems already exist, and creating sanctuaries and refuges) and surviving a collision if it does occur (again, by slowing boat speeds in certain areas). But let's be realistic—the continued expansion of boat speed regulatory zones and of manatee sanctuaries in perpetuity would be extremely distasteful to the waterborne community of Florida. The tough goal to reach will be to create some better balance between manatees' and other species' well-being and the ability of human users to enjoy many of the privileges to which they have become accustomed. That goal will be reached, it seems to me, by maintaining some of the existing management approaches, by carefully incorporating innovative technological advances, by better understanding what manatees perceive and how they react, and by working together.

It should be apparent that scientists still have just a rudimentary idea of what manatees can sense, as well as the nature of the cues that are truly meaningful to the animals. Part of the problem is simply the difficulty of obtaining meaningful data from free-ranging animals. I like the conclusion that Doug Wartzok and Darlene Ketten reached in their wonderful overview of marine mammal sensory biology:

One irony of sensory system research is that the more tools we invent to explore animals and their senses, the greater the hints that our reach is still too short. . . . Our greatest shortcoming is that we cannot yet measure or observe reliably and frequently in the truly relevant environment for marine mammals. . . . Until we do, we cannot truly understand what is happening in any marine mammal's ear, eye, or brain, and what transpires in the real world of most marine mammals . . . will remain a mystery.[2]

The reason all this sensory information is important is that only by understanding more fully what manatees see, hear, taste, and feel can managers and conservationists really make wise suggestions as to what people should do to help manatees make their way in an increasingly crowded world. Science doesn't provide the answers to managers and conservationists. Science provides knowledge that may help us to reach some balance between our own lives and activities and those of the wild species around us.

Partnerships and Sharing

THE YEAR WAS 1998: The Year of the Ocean. Across the United States, elected officials from the president on down, scientists, and the lay public celebrated a shared resource on which so many people depend. The federal government prepared a weighty compilation of information about uses of and cautions regarding the oceans and the living resources contained therein. Some of the figures and statistics were quite impressive:[1]

- One out of six jobs in the United States is marine-related;

- 180 million people visit our nation's coastlines annually, and travel and tourism represent both the largest and the fastest-growing segments of our country's service industry;

- over half of the population of the United States lives and works in coastal areas; by 2025 that proportion will reach 75 percent of the population;

- many coastal areas will become "sprawling, interconnected metropolitan centers";

- in both the United States and globally, fish and shellfish stocks are in decline and most fisheries are at or over their capacity;

- 40 percent of estuarine and coastal waters are neither fishable nor swimmable due to pollution;

- in 1996, bacterial contamination caused 2,500 closings and advisories for coastal bathing beaches; and

- the federal government cannot do all that needs to be done to mitigate damages and prevent problems of the future.

This somewhat frightening assessment becomes downright terrifying when one recalls that, in Florida at least, there will be more than twice as many people living in the state in 2030 as there were when the federal report was compiled. How can people maintain their quality of life while also preserving the natural resources that contribute mightily to that quality of life? As the 1998 Year of the Ocean report (under)states: "The federal government doesn't have all the answers."[2] The truth is that nobody does, and turning to our relatively few past successes for answers gives us astonishingly little insight to go on.

But that doesn't mean that there *are* no answers. Certainly humans are capable of learning from their mistakes (although they do not always do so!), and with this in mind, we may be able to discern some points of light.

What the Laws Say As has been noted in chapter 2, sirenians around the world are protected by international laws and agreements, national laws, and even regional and state laws. Here I shall comment simply on laws that cover manatees in the United States.

The State of Florida has had protective legislation for manatees since 1893, when people started to formally recognize that the species was becoming less and less common. The most recent state legislation to protect manatees is the Florida Manatee Sanctuary Act of 1978. This law considers the entire state to be a manatee sanctuary and provides managers for the state with the authority to designate particular locations as specially protected, even to the point where humans are prohibited from entering an area. Using the assumption that impacts to manatees are of greatest concern in 13 "key counties" where manatee numbers were considered to be the highest in 1978 or where manatee mortality was greatest at that time, the Florida Manatee Sanctuary Act also provides the state and counties with the authority to restrict boat access and speed to protect manatees in key locations. Pursuant to a directive in 1989 by the Florida governor and cabinet, the state assumed lead responsibility for developing most boat speed regulatory zones to protect manatees.

Sadly, neither the Florida Manatee Sanctuary Act nor the regulatory agencies have extended a strong focus to several other counties, despite post-1978 data that suggest high manatee numbers and human interactions in those jurisdictions. This law is often used in conjunction with another state law, the Local Government Comprehensive Planning and Land Regulation Act of 1985 (informally called the Growth Management Act). The latter legislation requires that all coastal counties develop and implement so-called manatee protection plans that attempt to reconcile future human population growth and the protection of manatees and other natural resources in Florida. Buoyed with good intent, the Growth Management Act has not been aggressively enforced, and many counties either lack approved plans or have had plans accepted that do not provide adequate protection. These laws are implemented more locally than is the case for the relevant federal laws.

On the federal side of the issue, there are two primary laws that protect manatees in Florida. The first is the Marine Mammal Protection Act of 1972, which provides protection for all marine mammals in waters of the United States. The goal of this act is to maintain marine mammal populations at their optimum sustainable population level, defined as a range of population sizes between the carrying capacity of the environment (K) and the maximum net productivity level (MNPL). Operationally, some have taken MNPL to be equivalent to about 60 percent of the carrying capacity. The Marine Mammal Protection Act prohibits the taking of marine mammals and defines taking to include harassment, hunting, capturing, killing, or *attempting* to harass, hunt, capture, or kill a marine mammal. Although harassment has been poorly defined (or enforced—or understood by the public), the term is generally taken by scientists and managers to mean causing changes in the "normal" behavior of a marine mammal or mammals. Feeding of free-ranging marine mammals is explicitly forbidden as a type of harassment (that is, a take). To date, one of the issues on which the act has been most effective is the identification and reduction of incidental taking of marine mammals in commercial fishing operations, which is not as serious an issue for manatees as it is for some other species.

The Endangered Species Act of 1973 is similar to the Marine Mammal Protection Act except that it covers only a subset of the marine mammals (only those designated as endangered or threatened)[3] and that it extends the definition of taking to include harming species; the term *harm,* in turn includes destruction or modification of "critical habitat" for a listed species or population. Violation of either act carries fines of up to $20,000 and a year in prison.

In cases where a human activity could jeopardize the continued existence of a species or population, a *Section 7 consultation* is mandated under the Endangered Species Act to assess the seriousness of the threat. Due to "aggressive" managers who used the power of the act as much as possible, through the mid-1990s more so-called jeopardy opinions were issued for manatees than for all other endangered species in the United States combined.

The listing of a species or population under the Endangered Species Act requires that the appropriate federal agency (for manatees, this would be the U.S. Fish and Wildlife Service) convene a Recovery Team to develop a Recovery Plan for that species or population. The creation of such teams and plans has provided tremendous opportunities for stakeholders representing various interest groups to come together, share opinions, and develop working relationships.

There are several other federal laws that do or can apply to marine mammals. The most important is the National Environmental Policy Act, a broad and important piece of legislation that has among its ambitious goals the following: "(1) [C]reate and maintain conditions under which humans and nature can exist in productive harmony; (2) fulfill the responsibilities of each generation as trustee of the environment for succeeding generations; (3) maintain, wherever possible, an environment that supports diversity; and (4) enhance the quality of renewable resources."[4] This act requires that environmental impact statements or environmental assessments be prepared when proposed actions are anticipated to have significant impacts on the quality of the environment.

Who Are the Players?

A variety of groups have played an important role in addressing issues associated with manatees in Florida. A cursory listing includes, but is not limited to, the following:

- *U.S. Marine Mammal Commission:* An independent federal agency with oversight for all marine mammal activities in the United States. The Commission was created and authorized by the Marine Mammal Protection Act. A great number of past manatee conservation initiatives occurred due to recommendations or actions by the Commission.

- *U.S. Fish and Wildlife Service:* The federal agency charged with conservation and management (including facilitating research, coordinating Recovery Teams, conducting enforcement activities) for manatees as stipulated under the Marine Mammal Protection Act. The Service conducts Section 7 consultations under the Endangered Species Act and manages national wildlife refuges. The Service is part of the Department of the Interior.

- *U.S. Geological Survey, Biological Resources Division:* Also under the Department of the Interior, this agency is charged with conducting and facilitating research on manatees. The Sirenia Project is now part of the U.S. Geological Survey, but was originally part of the U.S. Fish and Wildlife Service.

- *U.S. Army Corps of Engineers:* Responsible for permitting various human activities. The Corps has become involved in consultations regarding mitigation of manatee deaths in canal locks and flood control structures. The Corps has funded certain manatee research activities as well.

- *Other Federal Agencies:* The Cooperative Fish and Wildlife Research Unit, National Aeronautics and Space Administration, National Marine Fisheries Service, National Park Service, and U.S. Navy have all contributed to research relating to manatees or manatee habitat.

- *Florida Department of Community Affairs:* A state agency responsible for approving local management plans and developments having regional impacts.

- *Florida Department of Environmental Protection:* A state agency responsible for the use of state-owned lands and certain regulatory activities with relevance to manatee and habitat conservation.

- *Florida Fish and Wildlife Conservation Commission:* The state agency charged with research, enforcement, management, and conservation of manatees. The research is conducted primarily through the Florida Marine Research Institute in St. Petersburg. The Bureau of Protected Species Management (Tallahassee) conducts permit reviews and facilitates development of manatee protection plans and other management initiatives such as regulatory zones. The Division of Law Enforcement is located in Tallahassee as well.

- *Manatee Technical Advisory Council:* An independent group formed to provide advice to the executive director of the Fish and Wildlife Conservation Commission.

- *Oceanaria and Marine Zoological Parks:* Places such as SeaWorld, Miami Seaquarium, Disney's Living Seas, Lowry Park Zoo, and Homosassa Springs State Wildlife Park contribute such activities as conducting research on manatees, serving an important education function, and providing care and rehabilitation of diseased or injured manatees.

- *Mote Marine Laboratory:* This private laboratory conducts a wide range of research on free-ranging and captive manatees. Mote staff also assess effectiveness of regulatory zones and enforcement and assist with monitoring and recovery of diseased or injured manatees.

- *Power Companies:* Florida Power & Light Company has been an important part of research and education efforts statewide for almost three decades. More recently Tampa Electric Company has contributed to education and facilitated research in the Tampa Bay area. Reliant Energy (based in Houston, Texas) recently acquired plants in Florida and has shown signs of becoming an important contributor to research and planning efforts. Florida Power Corporation has recently been more active in discussions focused on the manatee–warm water issue.

- *Save the Manatee Club:* The club has been the primary nongovernmental environmental group involved in education, research, and litigation involving manatees in Florida for 20 years. Other groups include the Sierra Club, Ocean Conservancy, Pegasus Foundation, and Florida Audubon Society.

- *Colleges and Universities:* Individuals and programs at Eckerd College, University of Florida, University of Miami, Florida Institute of Technology, Howard University, University of South Florida, and Florida Atlantic University have conducted important research, contributed to education programs, or been involved with policy regarding manatees.

- *South Florida Water Management District:* The district has worked with the Corps of Engineers to try to resolve problems associated with entrapment of manatees in flood control structures and locks. It supports manatee research initiatives in southwestern Florida.

- *Marine Industries Association:* This group and others (such as Standing Watch) have participated in Recovery Teams and other integrative activities to represent certain constituencies that are concerned about the extent of restrictions on boat access and use.

- *Coastal Conservation Association:* A relative newcomer to manatee-related issues, but a powerful force in terms of maintaining recreational fishing. This group recently (2001) initiated a request for the state to reexamine whether manatees merit endangered status under state endangered species legislation.

The above list does not attempt to be exhaustive. It does attempt to show that a lot of groups are interested in or involved with manatees and in rules pertaining to manatee conservation.

Building Effective Partnerships

From sports teams to businesses, communication and coordination of effort are vital for success. When it comes to manatee management, I cannot recall a time in the past 28 years when communication and coordination were worse, when issues were so polarized, when misinformation was so rampant, and when anti-manatee feelings among the general public ran higher. It seems sometimes as if some (*not* all!) members of the media and others have worked conscientiously to prevent effective communication and coordination from happening by keeping the pot stirred with real and "enhanced" points of conflict. I guess that it just doesn't make good reading to discuss matters that provide unification and progress. But by accentuating differences rather than points of common ground, writers and others have driven a wedge into potentially productive communication among the various players. If one hears often enough that there can never be agreement over a set of issues, finally it may just make sense to stop trying.

There have been relatively few efforts to get a wide range of different stakeholders together to discuss the issues. To be sure, there have been occasions when different groups opposed one another during litigation, but conversations directed through attorneys just aren't the same as speaking directly and without the threat of legal action.

I recall my introduction to Pat Riley (no, not the basketball coach—this one is an influential and knowledgeable representative of marina development and management interests). Pat and I met while sitting across from one another at a table as part of an attempt for an out-of-court settlement that involved manatees in the Fort Myers area. It was not an ideal scenario for getting to know much about the rationale for our different thoughts or to gain a lot of interest in working together. Since that time, we have been thrown together on a Recovery Team, proposal review teams, and other venues where there has been time to talk and to learn from one another. It is extremely unlikely that Pat and I will ever agree on all the details, but we have come to like and respect one another, to be able to joke with each other, and to be able to work productively toward common goals. Who'd have guessed it!

The Marine Mammal Commission has attempted at its annual meetings to provide a forum for learning points of view from a variety of individuals and groups. In addition, the various iterations of Manatee Recovery Teams, Manatee Technical Advisory Councils, and other groups provide some productive chances for interactions among the different groups. Perhaps the most remarkable effort took place at the turn of the century.

On October 19, 2000, Florida's Governor Jeb Bush and his staff convened the Florida Manatee Summit to accomplish the following: (1) focus on key issues in manatee protection, especially access management; (2) identify challenges and opportunities for manatee protection from different perspectives; (3) explore the range of options available for solutions; and (4) discuss current and future roles for local, regional, state, and federal governmental agencies and private entities. To facilitate progress, a number of individuals were invited—absent staff lawyers—to represent a wide range of interest groups: 11 elected officials from the state government; 7 representatives of environmental groups; 6 individuals who represented boating access and fishing interests; 8 persons who head or otherwise speak on behalf of state and federal agencies; and 3 county representatives. Sitting around a set of tables, people who had sometimes been painted as polar opposites and implacable opponents talked with one another about their goals and interests; they asked questions and sought clarification; and in the end, they found unexpected levels of common ground regarding the need for several things, including but not limited to the following: (1) better enforcement on Florida's waterways, (2) funds to support enforcement, (3) better signage regarding regulatory zones, (4) pursuit of technological innovations that would reduce or prevent adverse effects of boating on manatees, (5) increasing, enhancing, or restoring seagrass beds and other habitat, and (6) better and broader education. Major points of contention existed to be sure, and they mostly involved specifics regarding access to waterways and marine facility siting plans. But on many, if not most, topics, a refreshing and to some an astounding amount of agreement and common ground was discovered that could, if groomed and nurtured, lead to better partnerships and progress.

The summit participants recommended that the group be brought back together to further refine their ideas. Unfortunately that has not happened. But the summit showed the very positive effects that can happen when a powerful individual such as the governor of Florida calls people together and asks them to discuss issues and seek solutions rationally and creatively. Not many individuals have the clout or the interest and track record in environmental issues to accomplish this on a widespread basis: Governor Bush, Congressman Bill Young, and senator and former governor Bob Graham are among the recognized leaders who have supported manatee research and conservation in the past, and they are among the leaders who can continue to help the folks in the trenches to work better together in the future.

It is also important to note that part of the reason for the success of manatee management programs to date is that they have involved shared commitment of federal and state partners. This partnership has, among other things, allowed programs for manatee management and research to be maintained in the face of funding changes from year to year. Other marine mammal species (for example, Hawaiian monk seals) have not historically been the beneficiaries of such collaboration. In my opinion, continuation or even improvement of the relationship between federal and state partners is vital to long-term protection of manatees and habitat.

Despite the lack of follow-up in the form of additional discussions, certain things did happen. Governor Bush noted that the recommendations of the summit "lay the groundwork for better protection of manatees while preserving Florida's traditional culture of recreational and commercial boating." He then included in his 2000–2001 executive budget proposal funds for new enforcement officers and enforcement equipment; a plan to increase fines for violating manatee and boating safety speed zones; money for grants to counties to complete their manatee protection plans; and continuation of funds for research and education.

Some time after the summit, I traveled with James "Buddy" Powell to Tallahassee to talk with Ted Forsgren, the executive director of the powerful Coastal Conservation Association, whose members worried that pending rules and regulations to protect manatees might seriously jeopardize their ability to engage in recreational fishing as they wished. Buddy and I started the conversation by noting that recreational anglers and manatee conservationists have a lot of fundamental interests in common; for example, if seagrass beds disappear neither manatees nor many species of fish will survive, so seagrass (and other habitat) protection should provide some reason for the two groups to work together.

Ted, a bright and savvy former fisheries biologist, agreed with our opening premises and in our subsequent discussion the three of us found other points of agreement (among them our disappointment with the lack of certain important analyses and population models)—and a few of disagreement as well.

But I left Tallahassee that day feeling as if Ted and I could talk frankly, honestly, and productively about issues.

Whether the players in the manatee soap opera talk because the governor mandates or requests it or because rational discussion simply works, it is vital that folks communicate. Because it is hard to establish a trusting relationship or a dialog with people that are portrayed by the media as one's enemies, the process needs some help from the press. Ultimately, frank and open communication is the best and possibly the only way to break the current logjam.

Unfortunately, marine mammal management at the start of the twenty-first century seems to be headed in another direction much of the time. "Management by litigation" has captured the time, energy, and money of those associated with the management of marine mammals—and other species—across the United States. The primary problems with this approach involve (1) the crisis-management response to the most pressing (read "potentially most expensive") of yesterday's and today's problems, (2) the consequent relative disregard of proactive, effective, and cost-effective solutions to problems of the next decade or decades, and (3) the loss of communication among litigants.

The latter was a high cost of litigation associated with recent suits by various environmental groups. Those suits alleged that neither the state nor federal agencies responsible for manatees were doing all that they could and should under relevant laws to protect manatees and their habitats. In part, at least, the suits were precipitated by the observation that leaders of those agencies were not acting as aggressively as had their predecessors, even though pressures were mounting in terms of expanding human activities detrimental to manatees and habitat. A good discussion of the history and effectiveness of manatee regulatory activities and of perceptions thereof appears in a dissertation and publications by Richard Wallace.

I do not argue the rectitude of the lawsuits. I maintain, however, that litigation should be a last resort because the detrimental fallout from litigation may be as serious as the problems that initiated the suits in the first place. In the case of the recent suits relating to manatees, I believe the settlement agreements were appropriate and, if consummated by actions, will provide important protections for manatees and for habitat critical to manatee protection. I also believe that the fears that many people and interest groups had and continue to have about the extent to which manatee protection will exclude people from places and resources they wish or need to use will not prove justified. I believe that procedures will continue to be used to try (sometimes successfully, sometimes not, depending on one's perspective) to be fair and to meet tough, conflicting goals. What I like to remember is that process is extremely important here—the end results, as I noted, may not always be pleasing for all involved parties, but if the process is fair and inclusive, I derive comfort from that.

It is very difficult, though, for some people to believe in the process any longer. The litigation has, among other things, fanned the flames of distrust and led to the promulgation of destructive and exaggerated rumors. It will take a long time for trust either in certain people and groups or in the process to be re-created. That distrust doesn't even have to be based on reality because we all know that perception is what counts; and the perception that certain groups or individuals are not trustworthy has led to a reality that will flavor and retard conservation of manatees in the future.

Management by litigation should *not* be anyone's goal. I recognize that sometimes groups or individuals feel that they have done all that they can outside of the legal arena and must ultimately resort to this option. In such cases, perhaps it is the only option left. But I continue to hope that *proactive, careful, and rational* approaches will, as a rule, take precedence over *crisis-oriented and emotional* ones. The beneficiaries will include the manatees.

The Burden of Proof

One of the subtle provisions of certain legislation, including the Marine Mammal Protection Act, is that the burden of proof in wildlife management and conservation should be on the user. Operationally what this means is that we should recognize that there are certain financial beneficiaries associated with most human activities that affect wildlife or habitat. The burden should be on those beneficiaries and other users to show that their activities do *not* unduly affect the resources, rather than on the general public or government agencies to show that the activities *do* affect the resources in unacceptable ways.

The burden of proof argument has the potential to be a powerful tool that could save taxpayers money and promote better partnerships. Alas, it is rarely suggested, let alone used.

Consider, for manatees, how effective imposition of the burden of proof on the user could be. It would place the burden on developers to provide support for studies to show that their proposed activities would not harm manatees, rather than on agencies to prove the opposite. It would place the burden on users of particular bodies of water to show that lack of speed regulations would have little or no impact on manatees or seagrasses, rather than, once again, on agencies using taxpayer dollars to show otherwise.

Some people will be quick, at this point, to note that offers from industry to support studies have occurred in the past, but that they are sometimes viewed with suspicion (recall the pervasive lack of trust I noted above). Would or should a reputable scientist accept money from "the other side"? Sure, he/she should as long as it is clear that the contractor will not exercise inappropriate control or censorship over the data, analyses, and publications thereof. It is even worth noting that recently the Coastal Conservation Association, frustrated that the relevant state agencies had not conducted or facilitated the development of an up-to-date model dealing with manatee population status, contracted with an independent scientist to do just that.

Should the regulatory agencies be taken out of the loop by such a process? Not at all. Imagine, however, the power associated with perceptions about research in which it is transparently clear that the following criteria existed:

1. Funds were pooled from both user groups and responsible agencies;

2. A request for proposals to address an issue was disseminated to all interested parties, rather than just to a few;

3. A panel of scientists *without conflicts of interest* judged the proposals on the basis of merit; and

4. A final report from the contractor was provided to the agencies and user groups, and was followed without censorship by a publication in the peer-reviewed literature.

The point is that even the partnerships that are emerging sometimes lack cohesion in terms of funding and responsibility. With trust and transparency, and with imposition of the burden of proof on the user, we can collectively do much better in terms of accountability, effectiveness, and cost-effectiveness.

Guidelines—What Individuals Can Accomplish

I advise students to be passionate about their work. In marine mammal studies, this passion often leads to their becoming advocates of something. That is all well and good, but advocacy, science, coastal development, and other activities associated with marine mammal issues *must* be done in an environment of honesty. Exaggeration and polarization of issues leave the public with little option other than seeming indifference.

Let me give an example of ways in which enthusiastic advocacy can be harmful. In Florida, people who frequent the waterways have witnessed growing numbers of manatees through the early 1990s for many parts of the state. That should be cause for celebration among conservationists and managers, and members of the public should become part of the celebration as well, since they are a part of any success that occurs. However, in their zeal to make sure manatees are protected in perpetuity, some conservationists forget to stop and celebrate and congratulate—they simply keep up the pressure that manatees are going to disappear unless people mend their ways—today.

Now I happen to agree that the long-term future of manatees and most other species depends on some changes in human behaviors and values as human populations escalate. But to the average fisherman or boater, who sees more, rather than fewer, manatees, the claim of imminent disappearance of manatees seems pretty untenable. In fact, it sometimes leads to open hostility and distrust because people don't understand why some conservationists never seem satisfied.

A better approach, it seems to me, would be one that balances congratulations about progress, education regarding honest, realistic long-term prognoses supported by good science, and engendering a spirit of cooperation. I know, I know . . . easier said than done! But it is still worth doing (or at least making the attempt) and is far better than doing nothing or most other approaches.

Other "players" also strain their own credibility with their statements or actions. Writers, for example, who claim that rising levels of watercraft-related mortality of manatees are due *solely* to rising manatee populations ignore the science that indicates that the largest manatee subpopulation, at least, is stable or even decreasing. In addition, stating that the cause of rising mortality is *simply* a result of population growth ignores the very real possibility that the mortality could be influenced at all by more boats, faster boats, hull design changes that permit boats to enter at high speed shallow areas occupied by manatees, and high levels of boater noncompliance with speed regulations in areas designed to protect manatees.

Even agency actions can strain credibility and relationships. The U.S. Fish and Wildlife Service, for example, commendably promoted the creation of the Manatee Population Status Working Group in order to use the best available science to develop recommendations for demographic and population criteria that, if met, could support downlisting of manatees to "threatened" status. The working group's recommendations, as originally developed and presented to the Service and the Manatee Recovery Team, were not adopted in early drafts of the Recovery Plan. The apparent inclination by the Service to modify and weaken the very recommendations that the Service specifically sought created suspicions and strained relationships that persisted to some degree even after the Service ultimately adopted criteria that were quite close to those originally recommended by the working group.

Finally, the scientists themselves need to work harder, I believe, to make their findings available *in a timely way* to the public through both peer-reviewed publications (which provide some reassurance that the science is of good quality) and publication vehicles more suited to the general public. Lack of timely publishing and sharing sometimes, inadvertently, creates suspicion that the scientists are hiding something or just protecting their jobs. Did I mention that there is a lot of distrust out there?

These examples represent just a few cases in which people or groups might reconsider their positions in order to promote better credibility and "team play." Let's move on to more positive points.

Another thing I tell students is that individuals can make a huge difference—for good or bad. Sometimes my sentiments get brushed off as cliché, but the reality is that there is simply too much evidence that individuals have made a difference to ignore it.

My favorite difference maker is probably a dogged, committed, and courageous woman who recently passed away at age 107. Marjory Stoneman Douglas will always be remembered for writing *The Everglades: River of Grass,* which helped promote support to protect the Everglades from development. Saving the southern part of Florida during a time of mind-boggling expansion and development seems like a pretty daunting task, doesn't it? But she persevered, much to the benefit of people six decades later.

So what makes an individual effective in making a difference? The adjectives I used above to describe Ms. Douglas certainly apply. But so do some others. Individuals who make a difference do their homework; they come prepared. And part of that preparation involves two specific things: (1) considering an issue from several points of view, and (2) coming up with workable and balanced solutions. It seems abundantly clear that anyone can examine an issue and list a series of problems—the difference makers are the rare ones who go the next step and offer workable solutions.

Another part of success involves looking ahead, being proactive. I have referred to crisis management and noted that it occurs when easy options no longer exist. Crisis management is generally expensive and restrictive. By dealing with issues before a crisis arrives, the number and types of options are generally greater, and solutions are considerably less painful, than is the case if people wait for a crisis to act. The old adage that an ounce of prevention is worth a pound of cure is absolutely true.

In a 1999 chapter, I outlined some other "ingredients" that are needed to ensure effective conservation of manatees.[5] Some of them have already been dealt with in this book, but for the sake of completeness, I provide the list here as well:

- Work cooperatively to develop a management approach/recovery program that meets as many goals of stakeholders as possible. Approaches that take advantage of the strengths and perspectives of many are better than a more limited approach.

- Deal with people honestly and sincerely. Recognize that all points of view may have merit and deserve attention.

- Avoid seduction by technology. Although technology may offer certain solutions, common sense and the development of fundamentally strong approaches are more useful.

- Create a value system that considers more than just economics. Resources have value simply because of their existence (existence value or intrinsic value).

- Acknowledge that wildlife management, to a large degree, involves management of human activities. It will be exceedingly difficult to resolve wildlife issues until we confront and start to deal with the reality that the fundamental problem for most wildlife populations today relates to too many people consuming too many resources for the carrying capacity of the globe.

- Be conservative and farsighted.

- Place the burden of proof on individuals or groups who stand to benefit most from the use of resources that affect the survival of manatees or other species.

- Be patient. The problems we face were not created overnight—nor will their solutions be.

- Don't be *too* patient. The clock is ticking . . .

A final point to mention is that we in the United States sometimes tend to get involved in our own admirable studies and forget that relevant work, from which we can learn a great deal, occurs elsewhere. For example, in chapter 2 I mentioned some of the groundbreaking insights that Helene Marsh and her colleagues developed thanks to their working relationship with Australian aborigines. Ongoing work in Belize, where boat traffic is minimal and habitat integrity is great, provides scientists with "control" situations that permit insight into boat-related issues in Florida. The point is that we can learn a great deal that may shed light on Florida manatee issues by looking elsewhere.

The problems of today sometimes seem insurmountable, even crushing. Those of tomorrow seem vague and hard to grapple with. But human history is filled with cases where people of good faith worked together to accomplish great things—that is what manatees, manatee habitat, people, and quality of life for people in Florida all deserve.

Developing a
Conservation Ethic

A GROUP OF EMINENT SCIENTISTS, economists, and social scientists from around the world recently opined, "the time has come to develop a different working relationship between people and natural resources."[1] They, like many others, have realized that the ways we do things, the assumptions we make, the risks we are willing to take, and the "costs of doing business" simply do not guarantee that living resources or human quality of life can be sustained. Such people realistically note that conservation problems tend to be social and economic, but that biologists are often expected to provide the fodder (in the form of data) to solve them. New partnerships, new approaches, and even new ethics must be involved.

Conservation seems often to be perceived as an imposed activity that restricts people from doing what they may wish. At best, it is a term that is usually only hazily understood or articulated. According to scientists Gary Meffe, Bill Perrin, and Paul Dayton, conservation involves a complex of insights and values. They note that

an ideal relationship between humans and nature would safeguard the viability of all biota and the ecosystems of which they are a part and on which they depend, while allowing human benefit, for present and future generations, through various consumptive and nonconsumptive uses. The challenge is to determine the appropriate balance between resource and ecosystem use on the one hand and the health and quality of human life on the other. But it must be remembered that human health and prosperity ultimately depend on healthy, functioning ecosystems.[2]

These same authors go on to describe the "amalgamation and integration of biological, ecological, economic, sociological, political and institutional knowledge that must be brought to bear on the many issues facing marine mammal conservation."

The above definition and description make it clear that conservation is not something that is done to thwart people, nor does it involve only biological or ecological perspectives. Conservation, done properly, is a human activity that benefits humans—as well as living and nonliving natural resources. Meffe and his colleagues make some general recommendations about approaches to conservation:

- The size of and resource consumption by the world's human population impair or prevent efforts to conserve.

- Scientists must have knowledge of species and ecosystems such that anthropogenic impacts do not exceed the natural boundaries of variation.

- Humans are components of ecosystems, and human interests must be recognized and represented in conservation decisions.

- Assessment of a resource and of effects of its use should *precede* such use or restrictions thereof.

- Communication is key.

Overarching these guidelines are three fundamental principles: the humility principle (recognizing that we, as humans, have limitations), the precautionary principle (proceeding cautiously and conservatively), and the reversibility principle (avoiding taking steps that lead to irreversible changes). Endorsement of these principles inherently means that certain values are also endorsed.

This may all seem like a lot of philosophical prose. Let's turn to something concrete. Good conservation in Florida should attempt to perpetuate productive inshore ecosystems forever. This perpetuation would permit people to enjoy some of the things they may have moved to Florida to experience in the first place: fishing, bird or dolphin watching, swimming, and tranquil boating. To achieve the goal of good conservation noted above, a variety of actions and values come into play. First of all, how can the goal be achieved if there are twice as many people fishing, twice as many boats, more pollution, more closures of shellfishing areas due to pollution, and much less habitat for fishes, birds, and other wildlife? And if the crowds, toxicants, and loss of resources occur, what does that loss lead to in terms of quality of life—human or otherwise?

Good conservation would attempt to bring together diverse data and diverse perspectives and to seek a balance. It would recognize that short-term economics associated with natural resource use may *not* ultimately (or even immediately) be what is most important to most people. Good conservation planning would incorporate more experts from the social sciences—economists, sociologists, anthropologists, political scientists—because conservation must provide for humans as well as for nature. Good conservation would help to order, or reorder, values and would attempt, within the limitations of knowledge and vision, to promote the uses of natural resources that would benefit the most people for the longest time.

It should be obvious that good conservation requires people to work together, to communicate their values, and to compromise. It cannot happen overnight—I've already discussed the nurturing that is needed to promote trust and team play. But our leaders should encourage it to occur quickly, or we return to crisis management, high costs, and loss of options.

Issues Facing Florida's Manatees and People

In this book and elsewhere, there exist discussions of "the boating issue" and the issue of power (and heat) production to save manatees in Florida. Clearly each presents some problems that need to be confronted and worked out. For example, boaters don't want or intend to injure or kill manatees, but boaters also do not want what they perceive as restrictions to their rights. Boating and its attendant industries produce millions of dollars and jobs, but Floridians place equally high value (according to one survey) on manatee conservation.

Clearly power companies do not want to imperil manatees by turning off warm-water resources the creatures need; neither can those companies afford to produce warm water (and pass costs of that production along to customers) simply to warm some manatees in winter. Another tough issue . . .

An even larger issue that occupies the newspapers in Florida as I write is Florida's tax structure. It would seem so easy, wouldn't it, to simply suggest that Florida allocate more funding and resources to conservation problems involving manatees? But it isn't so simple at all.

Unlike most other states (43 of them), Florida lacks a personal income tax. This means that Florida's infrastructure is dependent on other taxes, including those associated with tourists and development, neither of which is necessarily a good thing for sustaining wildlife populations. In addition, state and local taxes in Florida are much lower than the national average, and there have been minimal increases in tax burdens in recent years. Floridians' pocketbooks have had it relatively good, and I am grateful.

The discussions of tax reform, not unexpectedly, provide a forum for politicians to suggest cuts to certain areas and increases to others. Among other things, it seems as if tax rates may drop, but the breadth of taxable items and services may increase. It seems very unclear to me where matters will end—I'm certainly not an economist—but I hope that the decision makers will take the time to look at the future and the big picture, rather than playing off particular interest groups as sometimes occurs.

Now, Lord knows I am not excited about being taxed any more than I already am. But would I be more comfortable with the idea if it meant, for example, that natural resources could be better conserved and a very poorly rated state education system improved? Well, that's enough to make me think about it! In fact, there is ample evidence (for example, studies designed to assess people's willingness to pay; people's purchasing specialty license plates) that many citizens of Florida value natural resources and conservation sufficiently that they already do or would donate money if it led to better conservation.

The issue isn't just taxes and what they mean to me for the next few years.

The issue is creating a system that allows Florida's infrastructure to weather recessions and other problems, to create nationally distinctive programs in education, conservation, and other areas, and to promote what makes sense for quality of human and other life for the long haul. It may mean the pinching of purses in the short run, but I could be convinced that that's OK.

Why Save the Manatee?   It seems that people ask "What's in it for me?" when asked to step up conservation efforts for manatees or other species. The best answers appear in a decade-old essay by Daryl Domning.[3] Under contract from the U.S. Marine Mammal Commission, he developed a statement in which he outlined reasons why manatees should be saved. Most of them actually deal with benefits to humans, so the chapter provides a good response to the question "What's in it for me?"

In increasing order of importance, Domning listed the following reasons:

1. Manatees are an interesting esthetic resource that people enjoy watching. For many people, Florida would be a less interesting place without manatees.

2. Manatees consume exotic plants, thereby reducing weed growth. This provides an economic benefit and reduces the need for toxic herbicides.

3. Manatees may represent an important entity in healthy ecosystems in Florida. As mentioned earlier, manatee grazing may promote production in seagrasses and thereby affect overall ecosystem productivity (including productivity of commercially and recreationally important species).

4. In this age of genetic engineering, manatees, with their hodge-podge of adaptations, may serve as an important genetic resource for human health or other benefits.

5. Human mental health depends to some extent on healthy natural systems. Our natural affinity for living things has even developed its own name—*biophilia*—and it is manifest in our having pets, building birdhouses, visiting zoos, and other activities. Thus, manatee health and well-being go hand-in-hand with ecosystem health and well-being . . . which help maintain human health and well-being.

6. Humans have awesome ability to destroy nature and other things—but this ability carries with it a responsibility *not* to do so. Our species should exercise good stewardship.

7. What excuse could we possibly give our descendents if we did *not* save the Florida manatee?

Just Do It!   Marine mammals mean a lot to people these days. Florida is an affluent and beautiful state that attracts new residents by the score. But can marine mammals coexist with the population that demographers expect to occupy the state in a few years?

The issues are pretty clear, and a substantial body of data exists to shed light on the wisdom of particular options. Unlike the status quo for other issues in other places, the manatee issues are blessed with information and the attention of affluent stakeholders, including but not limited to the residents of Florida. Manatees have shown themselves to be adaptable and resilient in the face of human activities, and their life history attributes, relative to those of some other marine mammals, suggest a reasonable ability to recover. It seems to me that the necessary ingredients exist to solve the problems associated with manatees and their conservation, *if* the will to do so exists.

Sooner or later other states with other wildlife issues will be where we are in Florida with manatees today. In 2002, those states may seem less attractive to human immigrants than Florida, but soon factors such as space, fresh water, and quality living in Florida will be reduced. The other wildlife issues in other states will be important, too, but does anything capture the public imagination like a marine mammal?

So it seems as if Florida, in 2002, represents the ideal setting to test our resolve. If we can do the incredible balancing act in Florida to conserve and maintain manatee populations and maintain a quality human existence, it sends a model and a message of hope elsewhere. If not . . .

As they say in the Nike commercials, let's "just do it!"

Mysterious Manatees

When I started writing this book, I wasn't too fond of the title. It seemed like just another gimmick to perpetuate some warm, endearing human feelings regarding marine mammals—right up there with the friendly dolphins, the gentle giants, and the adorable seals. Don't get me wrong: I like marine mammals a lot and have devoted my professional life to studying, conserving, and educating people about them; but dolphins have killed people, some whales play pretty rough, and seals bite like hell. Let's be honest (a recurring theme of this book): marine mammals may be a lot of things, but they rarely exhibit the human traits we arrogantly believe and wish they (and other species) should.

So, mysterious manatees? Well, I had to wonder about that title. But as I completed the book I became more comfortable with it. The haunting photographs of Karen Glaser set a quiet and somewhat mysterious tone. And the manatees themselves, as I think about it, have done some pretty mystifying things. They have survived and even, in some locations, continued to prosper in the face of a dramatically changing world. As long-time manatee biologist Bob Bonde likes to say, "The more I see of these animals, the more they amaze me."

What I like most about manatees is that they are so unlikely! As I have studied their various anatomical systems, I have been impressed, as Charles Darwin was with orchids, that manatees are an incredible assemblage of jury-rigged systems, collectively working wonderfully. In a more scientific sense, I love how far derived they are from their ancestral roots, how subtly almost every organ and system has its own special sirenian stamp. What amazing creatures to have evolved 50 million years ago!

And what amazing adaptations to permit manatees to live in the heart of civilization, in an environment foreign to what they encountered for the first 99.9998 percent of their existence on earth. One expects such survival and flexibility of cockroaches, cats, and coyotes. But the lumbering manatees?

I admire whatever it is about them that permits them to adjust, to persist, and to survive far longer than humans have on this earth.

Bud Freeman stopped by my office the other day just to chat awhile. We covered a few topics, but inevitably the conversation turned to manatees. We talked about the whereabouts of "our" tagged manatees in southwestern Florida, about the number of dead manatees recovered to date, and about the blessings of a relatively mild winter. Scientists have learned so much about manatees over the past 25 to 30 years. What we haven't learned—what remains a puzzle—is how manatees have persisted as well as they have and what the future holds. Mysterious manatees . . .

part II

Introduction to the Photographs

Karen Glaser

When I received a small yellow Instamatic underwater camera for a birthday gift in 1983, I began photographing children at play in the water. I was fascinated by the magnification and exaggeration of their bodies created by looking through water: their lean limbs elongated, their round figures inflated like balloons. Although these images of the children—resulting in a series of photographs entitled "Aquanauts"—did not begin as a serious photographic venture, the results of my experimentation changed the direction of my life as a photographer.

It was a natural shift for me to begin shooting the majority of my photographs underwater, as I've been an avid lover of water my whole life, enthralled by its force, power, and beauty. I also understand the essential nature of water for all life on Earth. Seeking these same qualities in my quest for underwater subjects, I came upon the idea of photographing manatees in 1992, when my former scuba instructor, Tom Gilchrist, described them. I pictured their body shapes as akin to the grand balloons at the Macy's Thanksgiving Day Parade. Therefore, my initial visual attraction to the manatee was in line with my previous work on the stretched and ballooning forms of people underwater. Tom informed me that Crystal River, in west-central Florida, was where I needed to go to find manatees, which is exactly where my husband, John, and I first encountered these fascinating animals.

Experiences with the Manatees

The first time that I swam with manatees I wasn't quite sure what to expect. John and I were told that they would not hurt us, that they are gentle and curious, "like 1,000-pound puppies." Unlike puppies, however, manatees are endangered. When I first began my manatee adventure, Florida law and accepted manatee etiquette prevented a person from initiating contact. This rule was deemed necessary to prevent humans from harassing the animals.

You could be near a manatee, but you were not allowed to approach the animal first. Luring them with food was also forbidden.

My introduction to manatees was a startling but thrilling experience. The first manatee approached me by coming quietly out of the mud (much of the Crystal River is crystal in name only). Then, feeling something under my fin, I looked down and discovered three huge manatees underneath me. My heart began pounding fast. By turns, the creatures frightened, excited, inspired, soothed, and, most of all, humbled me. And in time, as I relaxed around them, I realized how funny and affectionate these mammals can be.

During my years of photographing manatees, I have grown close to the good people at the Best Western in Crystal River and the Crystal Lodge Dive Center where I make my base. The operators of the dive shop trust me and know that I am careful. We leave their dock at daybreak before many boats are on the river. In our wetsuits, John and I load the boat with my cameras and other gear, including the snorkeling equipment that we use in lieu of the bubble-producing scuba regulators that scare manatees away.

As the sun rises, often a beautiful steam wisps off the warm river surface into the cooler ambient air of the morning, which usually hovers between 45° F and 55° F, although we have been out when it is as cold as 19° F. The time of the year to see manatees in large numbers is late fall to early spring. It is during this season that they congregate in the spring-fed rivers that emerge from the earth at about 72° F year round. The manatees hover over the springs for warmth, before scattering as the air warms to feed on aquatic freshwater plants throughout the river.

Usually John guides our boat, while I keep a watchful eye for manatees. The three main areas we explore in Crystal River are the Big Spring (also called King or Main Spring), Gator Hole (now renamed Magnolia Springs so as not to scare anyone), and Three Sisters. Throughout Crystal River are manatee sanctuaries cordoned off where the manatees may swim and people may not venture. Big Spring can be either clear or cloudy and stirred, depending on the activity of the assembled creatures. Besides manatees, this spring attracts mangrove snappers, mullet, sheepshead, and by far the largest, most exquisite tarpon I have ever seen. At times as I swim in this area I will catch a bright flash out of the corner of my eye; it's the light hitting the gigantic sequined scales of this formidable fish.

Much of the spring at Gator Hole is a sanctuary. The portion of Gator Hole where people are permitted to swim is murky. For that reason, this can be a challenging but fun place to photograph, because manatees sneak up and surprise me, appearing from out of nowhere.

The entrance to Three Sisters is where photographers most frequently shoot pictures of the manatee. The water is generally clear and shallow, and in the cool morning large numbers of manatees often bask in the water's relative warmth. Beyond the entrance is a shallow channel that leads to the three distinct springs for which it is named. When the water is low, a strong current usually comes down the channel. Manatees do not fight the current to swim upstream, into the springs. When the incoming tide deepens the channel water, manatees venture up the narrow passage. At these times, there may be many manatees in these beautiful waterways.

The mammals may have the water stirred up so that visibility is next to nothing. It's exciting because I can feel their presence but can't see anything; so, suddenly, in a great cloud of turbid water, I realize there are manatees all over the place. On other occasions the water is breathtakingly clear. When this happens, a swimmer may be lucky enough to see a bream-filled spring with a manatee quietly asleep on the bottom. The manatee surfaces periodically, effortlessly, as if suddenly filled with helium, to take a breath and then gently touches back down and continues his or her nap. When active, a manatee breathes every minute or so, but when at rest it may stay underwater for up to 20 minutes. One might also see a manatee hanging among the bream like a zeppelin in the sky.

The remaining spring, my favorite of the three, is lush with a jungle-like growth. It could easily be a set for a Tarzan movie. Above the water, I might see a great blue heron standing regally, surveying the spring from its edge. Under the water, it is often muddy and spooky. But if the water is clear, I might spy a cormorant diving down under the surface, playing tag with jacks as they chase each other. I feel joy and a quiet peace when I see these things.

Almost immediately after I started photographing manatees in Crystal River, my visual attraction to them turned to one of concern. Interacting with them, I noticed how many manatees bore terrible scars. Many had been hacked and cut by propeller blades. Others had had unfortunate encounters with fishing apparatus, crab traps, fishing line, locks, and flood gates. The most chilling thing I saw was a manatee with initials carved in his hide. In fact I learned the scarring is so pervasive that scientists use this scarring to identify individuals.

In developing our coastal areas throughout the Americas, we have encroached on the manatees' habitat. Loss of habitat is the worst problem facing these mammals. This problem is widespread both in the United States and in Central and South America. Furthermore, we put manatees at risk when we behave wildly on waterways, as if no fellow creatures live below. Consequently, their status as an endangered species, in large part, rests on our collective shoulders. Accordingly, my concern for the manatees' welfare became a guiding force behind my photographic work, and I felt compelled to learn more about them.

The Habitat of the Florida Manatee

As I understand it, the Florida manatee can regularly be found along the Atlantic coast from Georgia down to Miami, and along the Gulf Coast from the Everglades up to St. Marks in the Florida panhandle. The highest count of individual Florida manatees in 2001 was 3,276. The Florida manatee can exceed 13 feet in length and weigh over 3,500 pounds. Manatees swim in both fresh and salt water. During the summer months they scatter to the warm waters of the Gulf of Mexico and the Atlantic Ocean, but they are extremely sensitive to cold water and can die from hypothermia. During the autumn and winter months when coastal waters chill, some manatees migrate to inhabit Florida's spring-fed rivers, where the temperature remains warm. (Manatees will also venture to the warm water around power plants.)

Florida has an enormous underground aquifer, or freshwater reservoir. It is the "overflow" from this aquifer that produces an elaborate, warm, freshwater spring system throughout the state. These springs keep the rivers temperate, and this unique environment offers a refuge to large numbers of manatees in the winter. Crystal River's warm temperature and its close proximity to the Gulf make it a key destination for wintering manatees.

Crystal River is a small, friendly community in Florida, about 90 miles north of Tampa and nine miles from the Gulf. There are large, lovely homes on its riverbanks where people enjoy watching birds such as ibis and pelicans in their backyards. The river is a wildlife refuge, so these beautiful birds can also be seen in and around the many mangrove, cypress, and palm trees that are on the river's shore. As on many Florida rivers, there is a marina housing pleasure boats. The town of Crystal River is like many Florida communities. In the malls are Eckerd Drug, Publix and Winn Dixie grocery stores, as well as the local barbecue (in this case Fat Boys, and pretty good, too), JCPenney, marine supply stores, dive shops, and so on. The big difference is that people come to this community from all over the world to swim with manatees. Crystal River is an enormously popular freshwater dive site. It is known as *the* place to see manatees. A thriving tourist industry has grown from this town's unique situation.

For better or worse, manatees in recent years have become the "Barney" of the animal kingdom. People see them as adorable in an ugly sort of way. Their head is like a Chinese Shar-Pei with a potato body and spatula tail. On a winter weekend, people can be on the Crystal River in droves to get a glimpse and feel of these creatures. Busloads of schoolchildren are even brought down from neighboring states. Many of the manatees are socialized and appear to enjoy the attention and touches of humans, while others avoid people. So, to protect their privacy, manatee sanctuaries—where humans are forbidden—were created in the river. The local dive shops are required to show a videotape on manatees and on how humans must behave around them before allowing their customers on the river. People are generally respectful of these boundaries, and those who ignore them and enter the sanctuaries can receive a steep fine.

About seven miles down the road from Crystal River is Homosassa Springs State Wildlife Park. Rescued manatees live at this park in captivity. They are in a natural part of the river that has a barrier in it so they may not venture out. They happily get fat on mass quantities of romaine lettuce and carrots. The animals are well cared for, and there is an education program about the animals at the park. This park also is home to other wildlife, many native to the area such as alligators and others imported such as the hippopotamus. Homosassa River has many wild manatees in it as well.

Swimming with manatees is controversial. Based on the Marine Mammal Protection Act, the interpretation of the law governing manatee and human interaction has changed. The way the law is now interpreted by at least some agency legal counsels, it is illegal to touch the animals, no matter who initiates the contact. The concept is to appreciate wildlife from a distance as we do when we bird-watch. The difference is that many of the manatees enjoy touching you, and insist that you touch back. Some scientists and environmentalists believe that this interaction truly makes a positive mark on our behavior, while others feel that this is inviting an unhealthy dependence on humans and possible harassment of the animals. What should swimmers do if a manatee approaches them? It is a complex issue. As one scientist suggested, perhaps the enforcement of this law will be based on the behavior of swimmers and their ability to respect the space surrounding this precious mammal.

About the Manatee

As John Reynolds explains in detail in his wonderful text, manatees are large, herbivorous, aquatic mammals. The most common animal that they are related to, in terms of how a layperson might see a resemblance, is the elephant. The Florida manatee is a subspecies of the West Indian manatee. This creature is one of the four surviving species of the order Sirenia, along with the dugong and the Amazonian and West African manatees. They are generally not aggressive and have a gentle disposition. Along with the threats previously mentioned due to loss of habitat, their gentle nature has historically put them in danger from hunters. They were easy prey for explorers and still are for indigenous people in some developing countries. They are big creatures and their meat is said to be delicious.

Manatees are semisocial. They spend their days eating, sleeping, playing, and traveling. The average manatee in captivity eats about 80 pounds of vegetation a day; this amount may vary a bit in the wild. They help keep some rivers free of some water-choking nuisance weeds. Some favorite foods of wild manatees include hydrilla, eel grass, water hyacinth, manatee grass, and turtle grasses.

There is a manatee in captivity at the South Florida Museum, Bishop Planetarium, and Parker Manatee Aquarium in Bradenton, Florida, that is over 50 years old. Scientists suspect that manatees can grow as old as 60 years or more if not prematurely killed by a human. Manatees become sexually mature somewhere between two and about five years. A mating herd forms when a female is in estrus and there is a lot of physical activity. It is not known how many males she may mate with, but the males do not get aggressive toward one another or fight. The gestation period for the female is about 12 months, and she may calve every 2.5 years. Manatees usually deliver a single calf, but they are known to bear twins.

Manatees chirp and squeak. The animals presumably make these sounds to maintain contact with one another and to indicate particular emotional states such as fear or alarm. Mothers and their calves are frequently heard responding specifically to one another based on sound. A recent study suggests that individuals have distinctive acoustic characteristics to their calls, suggesting that some manatees can recognize each other as individuals based on vocal cues.

The Photographs

I consider my work to be environmental portraits. When I photograph manatees, I try to be as patient, careful, and respectful of the animals as possible. I hold both a bachelor's and a master's of fine arts degree, although I was never trained specifically in underwater photography nor was I trained as a biologist. My underwater photographic process is somewhat different from the method most underwater photographers prescribe. Most of the underwater photography that one sees is in color. The full-color spectrum, however, is lost 10 feet down. Photographs taken below this point in natural light generally have a heavy blue or green cast. Traditional underwater photographic training advises using color film with a flash to "regain" color. Consequently, the flash is held at a distinct angle to avoid backscatter from particulate matter in the water. The problem with this method is that the flash photographs shot underwater often look artificial, and reminiscent of Las Vegas glitz. (This is not to say that there are not exquisite underwater photographs made in color by excellent photographers.)

To avoid this unnatural look, and to capture my experience with the manatees in an often murky environment, I photograph in black-and-white, relying only on natural light, and I sometimes subtly "color" the pictures later through toning (plates 40, 41, and 49). After all, the manatees are grey in grey water.

The subtleties of the light in my pictures are from the variations in the light as it filters through the water's particulate matter. This muck seasons the soupy, magnificent underwater light. It is not the color but the light surrounding the forms of the manatees that is the essence of my photographic experience. To accentuate further the feeling of the water and light gracing and embracing these large aquatic mammals and their environment, I shoot my photographs with a grainy film and later enlarge the prints to 30 by 40 inches. I want to show the viewer their behavior in and harmony with their habitat. I also hope the viewer picks up on the "punch" the photographs sometimes deliver. What I mean by punch is that I will engage the viewer with a beautiful photograph, but the scars that the manatees carry on their bodies are ever-present reminders of human impact. I want the images to win people's hearts and make them think about our relationship to these magnificent creatures and to their habitat. To my mind, the interdisciplinary nature of this project has been its strength and is an important source of power for people who view it.

Colombia   Although this book features the manatees of Florida, I visited Colombia in 1997. In the United States, I had met Juan Alberto Gaviria, the gallery director of Centro Colombo Americano, an important cultural center in Medellín. He responded well to my work and organized a large exhibition of these photographs in his gallery. He also invited me to visit Colombia, where he arranged two trips so that I might begin to learn about the efforts being made in his country on behalf of the manatee.

The first area I traveled to, on this journey to learn about manatees in Colombia, was Magangué in the Department of Bolívar (equivalent to an American state). This is an agricultural area at the junction of the Cauca and Magdalena Rivers 120 miles southeast of Cartagena. My understanding is that this is also the largest *ciénaga* (marsh or swamp) area in Colombia. There are Antillean manatees here. The Florida manatee and Antillean manatee are the two subspecies of the West Indian manatee. At the opening of my exhibit in

Medellín I met Ricardo Botero, who hosted my visit in Magangué. Ricardo was a rancher in Magangué who had residences there and in Medellín. He had studied animal science at the University of Florida. Ricardo related to me that, during a long hot summer sometime in 1973, he came to Magangué and noticed that the people of the region were catching the manatees, killing them, and consuming their meat. At that time he became worried about the species. The fishermen said that their communities were very impoverished and that they could feed a lot of people with the meat.

In 1986 he started a campaign to educate the local fishermen about the importance of the manatees to the ecosystem and why they should preserve this species. He tried to convince the fishermen that, if they caught a manatee, they should return it to the river.

In 1992, Ricardo and a local high school biology and chemistry teacher, Rafael Vidal, officially started the foundation Amigos del Manatis to educate the community about manatees and the environment. Rafael enlisted the help of his high school students to learn about the mammals, to exchange information, and to carry what they learned back to their communities. At a certain point Ricardo and his team were visited by an environmental official from the government who saw their work, praised their conservation efforts, and said that he wished there were more people like them. In 1997, at the time when I visited Ricardo Botero's ranch, there were 12 manatees in the lake. Of the 12, he had seen 3 born there. Most important, however, 2 of the 12 manatees had been donated by fishermen. Amigos del Manatis's message about the manatees' importance to the local ecosystem was being heard.

While I was in Magangué, Rafael Vidal and other townspeople took me to the lake where the manatees live. One young man put me in a wooden canoe on the lake. They threw water hyacinth in the lake to try to rustle up a manatee for me to see, even though, in my broken Spanish, I tried to let them know that, while I appreciated their efforts, it wasn't necessary. When anyone thought they saw a manatee there was dead silence; no one moved because

the manatees would flee if they heard a noise. It was a chilling realization.
I was so used to the manatees back at Crystal River, where sometimes they
would frolic with tails slapping; certain manatees would even appear to greet
the boat. At least you would see the manatees come up for air or roll in the
water. It doesn't happen in the wilds of Colombia. Manatees there seem to
know that if they appear they might get harpooned.

I spoke again with Ricardo Botero in 2002 while preparing this essay. It
was wonderful to hear that Amigos del Manatis is still up and running and that
its conservation efforts continue. Recently it worked with two governmental
organizations to facilitate the donation of two pairs of manatees to two different Colombian national parks. Educational programs have been developed at
both of these locations to raise public awareness about this species.

The second place I visited in Colombia where manatees lived was the Amazon. I stayed at a national park, Amacayacu, which is between Leticia, the port
where people embark for the Amazon, and the small town of Puerto Nariño.
Amazonian manatees are very elusive. The indigenous people in this area hunt
them as well. My hope was to meet a scientist who worked at a research station at Puerto Nariño called Fundación Omacha. I was told that this scientist
had done a great deal of research on the pink dolphins of the Amazon and was
now starting to research the Amazonian manatee. Unfortunately, it turned
out that the scientist was in Scotland, but I was able to see and swim in the
very muddy Amazonian environment where the manatees might be found.
I was also able to visit the research center, which turned out to be a lovely
wooden house on the banks of the Amazon. Through a friendly park employee
who knew some English, I spoke to a biologist at the center. I know some
Spanish and I heard her say "*cinco carnes.*" I asked the young woman who was
helping me with translation to ask her again what she meant. She said that the
indigenous people eat the manatees; they say manatees have five kinds of meat
the way chickens have two. I recently asked a scientist back in the United
States about this and he said, yes, they have at least that many kinds of meat.

Once again I was struck with the difference in the behavior of the manatees in Colombia and those in Crystal River. Many of the manatees in Crystal River have become very socialized; in the Amazon they hide. In some twisted sense the manatees in Florida don't know how good they have it, only being hit by boats and such.

Conclusion Ultimately, this project challenged me, first as an artist and second as an interactive participant in the marine environment. My experiences swimming with and photographing manatees have broadened my understanding of our interdependence with these and other creatures. How we choose to use our wetlands and coastal environments should express our human creativity and potential. Our use of these areas should reveal our sensitivity to the idea that we share these places; we do not own them. Marine biologists and ecologists view the manatee as an indicator species in the coastal waterways because it is so highly susceptible to how humans use and abuse this environment. I have often heard them referred to by scientists as the canary in the coal mine. To quote Juan Alberto Gaviria, the curator of my manatee exhibition in Colombia: "Man should be conscious that he is not the only beneficiary of this planet; moreover, to be a beneficiary requires a learning process of coexistence with other species."

I see this project as my dialogue between two species—human and manatee—in which my work unites art, spirit, and science. My goal is to make elegant photographs of this unique marine mammal that will move viewers and interest them in learning more about manatees and their habitat. I hope that my work will propel others to join the effort to preserve these creatures and their home. If my art can affect people in so positive a manner, then I have a satisfaction about doing my part toward enhancing public education and conservation.

1. I call this picture *Elephant's Cousin*, because a manatee is an elephant's cousin and this picture shows the resemblance. 1993.

2. Crystal River. 1994.

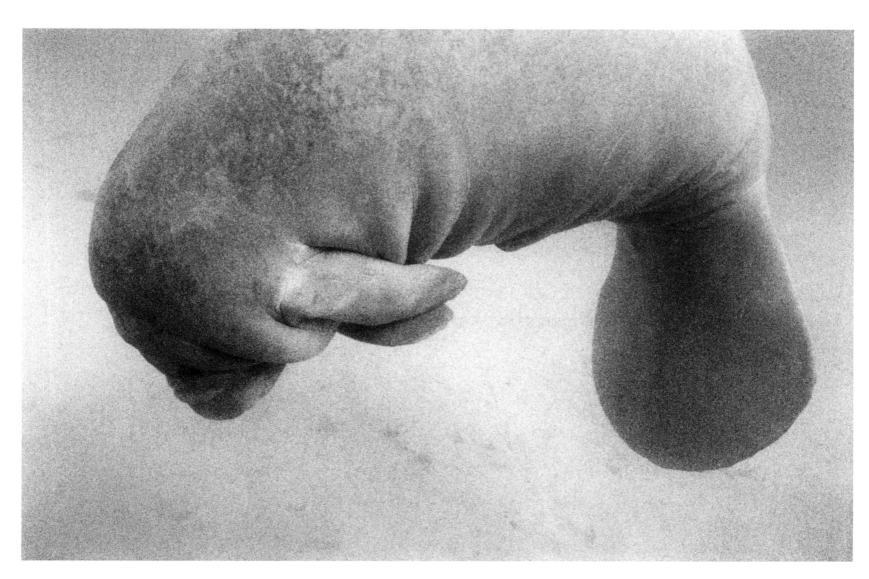

3. Crystal River. 1995.

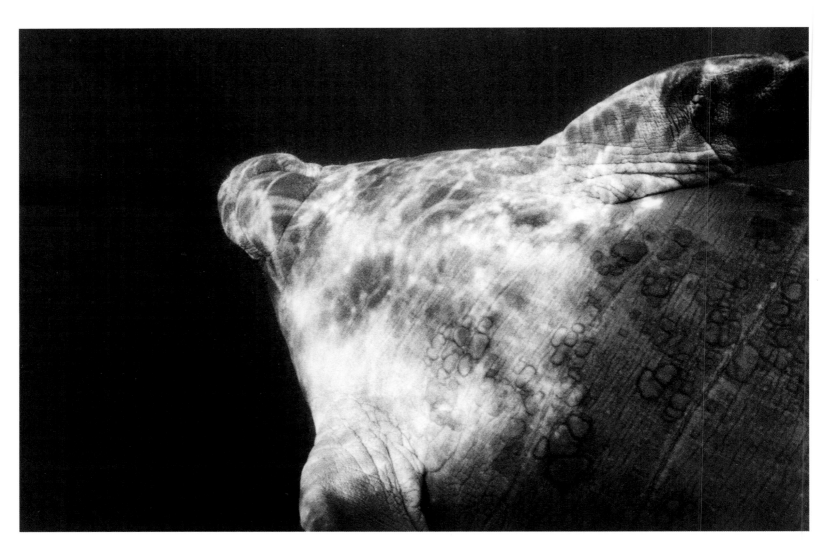

4. Crystal River. 1995.

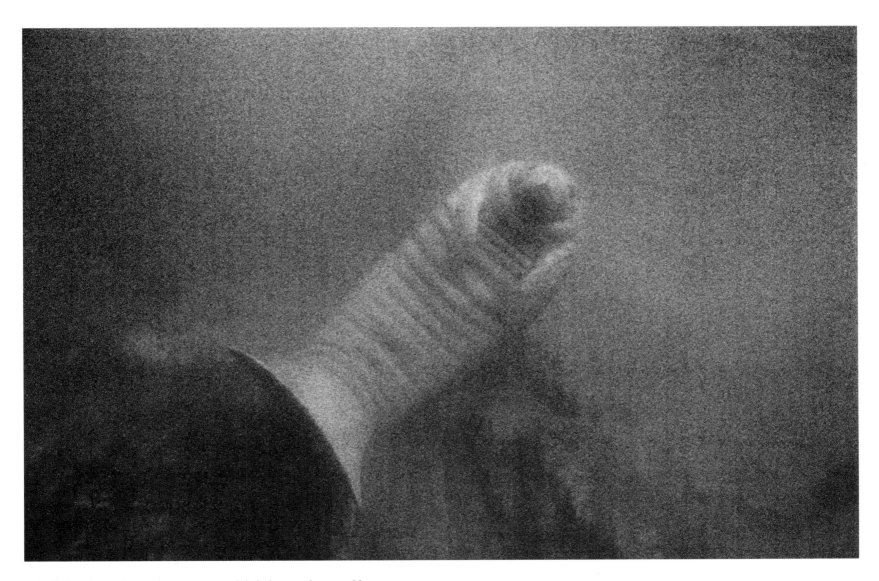

5. I call this picture *Mummy*, because one can't help but see the resemblance. 1997.

6. Crystal River. 1994.

7. Crystal River. 1993.

8. I was at Gator Hole, and I could barely see in front of me when this mama and baby appeared from the blackness with another manatee close behind. 1995.

9. I visited Crystal River in November. The visibility was the worst I'd ever experienced. I was up to my eyes in water and up to my knees in muck. Boiling from the mud, a manatee suddenly appeared. 1994.

10. Jesse White, who had been the veterinarian at the Miami Seaquarium for years, loved manatees. I had the honor of meeting him at his home early on in this project. This picture was his favorite. 1993.

11. The deepest spring at Three Sisters was so peaceful and clear this day. 1995.

12. Crystal River. 1995.

13. Crystal River. 1994.

14. Manatees surface to breathe and frequently swim at the top of the water. This is when they get nailed by boats. 1993.

15. It was a crisp, cloudy morning when I saw these manatees playing in the distance. The center manatee in the picture saw me and made a beeline toward where I was swimming. His companions followed. As the manatees reached me, the sun came out. 1995.

16. It's beautiful to watch the manatees curl and make abstract shapes with their bodies in the diffused light. 1996.

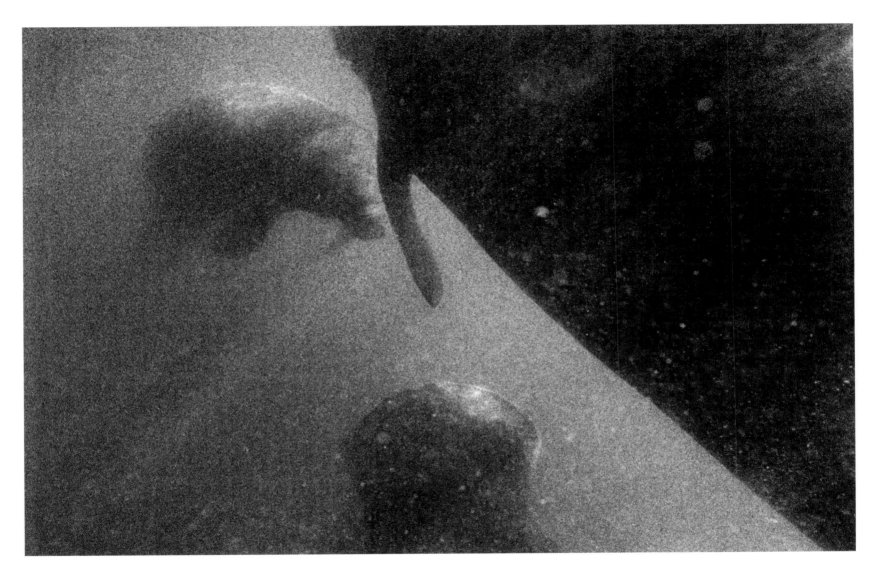

17. Crystal River. 1997.

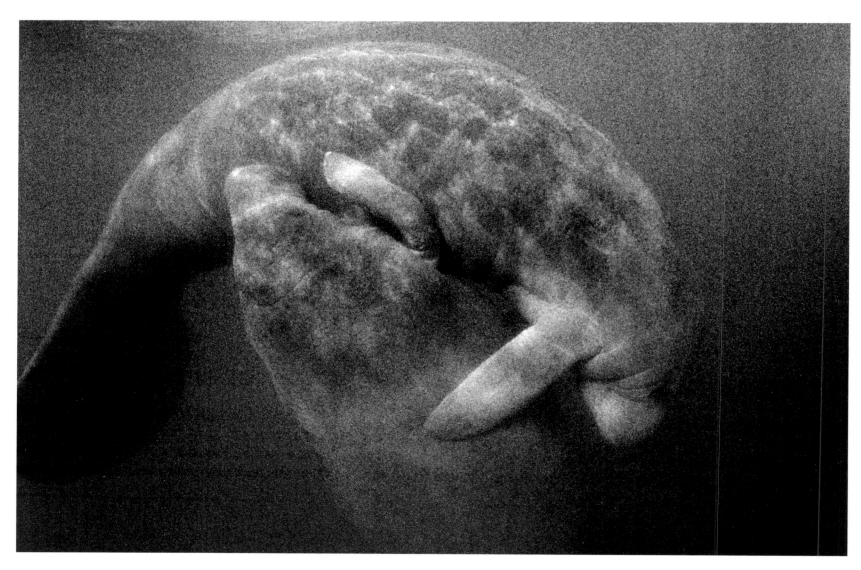

18. One of my favorite pictures. 1996.

19. I used to call this image *Dugong Tail*. This manatee's fluke was damaged by a boat propeller. The V-shaped fluke resembles that of its cousin, the dugong. Now I title it *Amee's Favorite* after one of my former assistants who was crazy about the photograph. 1995.

20. Manatees seem to enjoy touching and nuzzling. 1995.

21. I call this picture *Bad Design*, because I break a "classic" rule of artistic composition by cutting everything off at the edges. Breaking the rules can work, though. 1996.

22. A manatee's fluke with sheepshead. 1998.

23. The manatees on the right are a nursing mother and calf. 1995.

24. I call this picture *Adrienne's Favorite* after Adrienne Bolsega, a fellow photographer who was moved by this image. 1995.

25. For some reason I think about the words "huddled masses" on the Statue of Liberty when I look at this picture. 1996.

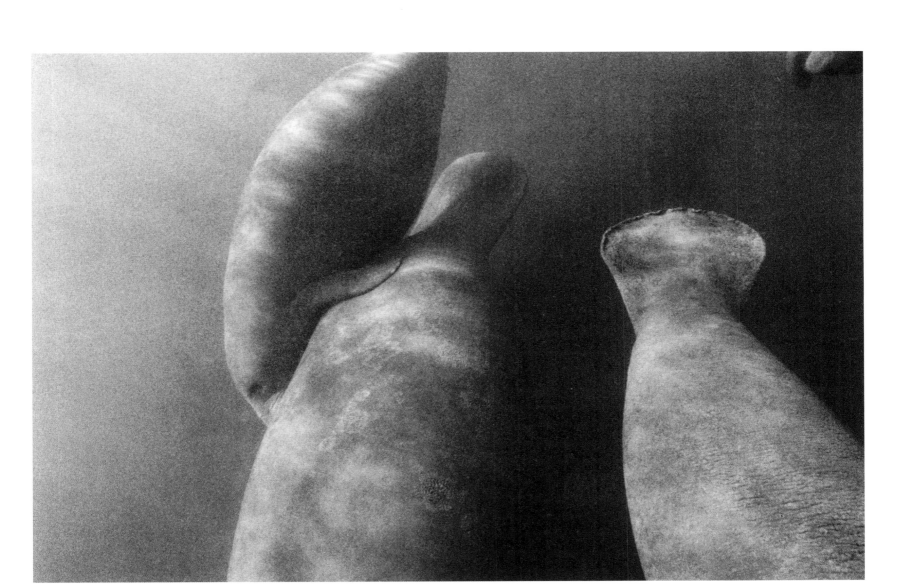

26. As you leave the dock at the Crystal Lodge Dive Shop and head out to the big spring you pass Banana Island. This is shot behind the island. 1993.

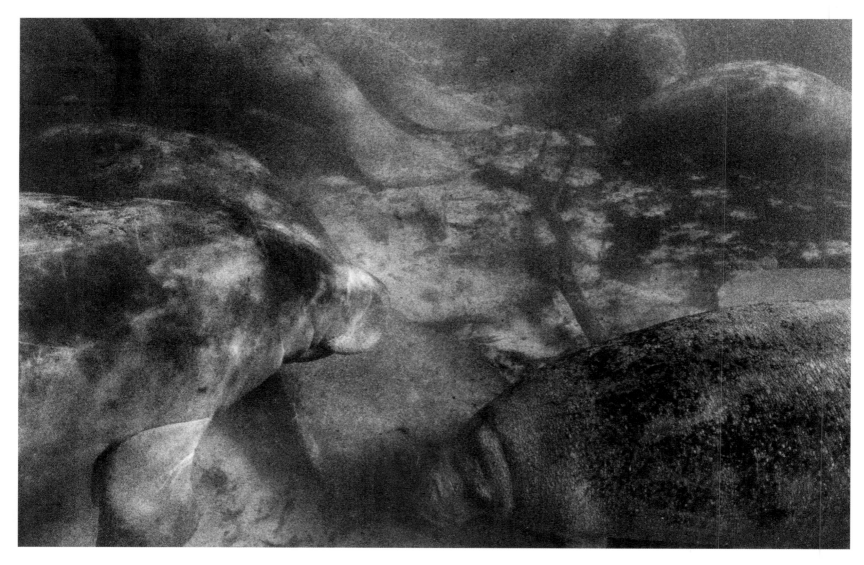

27. Crystal River. 1998.

28. The air temperature was 19° F this day. It was so cold that the boat rope was stiff with ice. Lots of manatees warmed themselves at the main spring. 1996.

29. Crystal River. 1995.

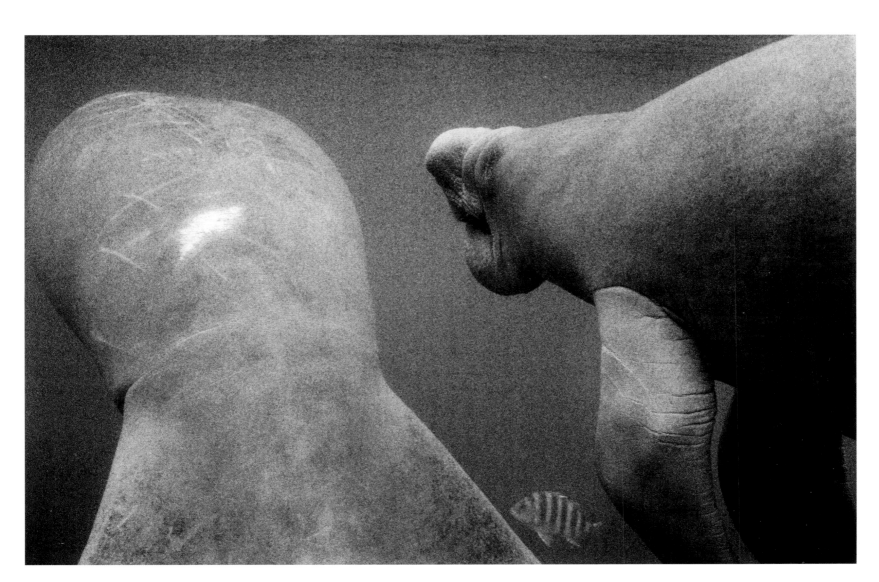

30. Crystal River. 1995.

31. This manatee's flipper may have gotten caught in a crab trap line. 1995.

32. The fluke of the manatee on the right is a strong reminder of the severe disfigurement that can be caused by a boat's propeller. 1998.

33. A manatee and diver. 1993.

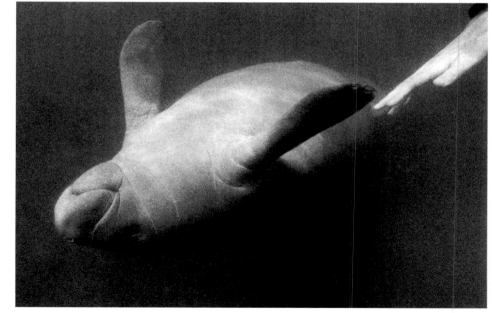

34. This baby manatee followed my friend Mary and me for about half an hour under its mother's watchful eye. We tried to swim away, but the young manatee persisted. One doesn't want to anthropomorphize too much, but eventually the mother let out a call that sounded like "Kid, get over here now," and the kid obeyed. 1994.

35. A manatee swims up to our boat early in the morning. Manatees frequently greet you in Crystal River, but manatees wouldn't dare do so in unprotected areas such as the ones I visited in Colombia. 1995.

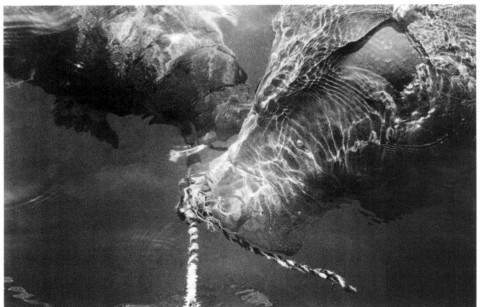

36. We frequently see manatees chewing on our boat rope. We wait until they leave before turning on the motor. 1995.

37. I really like this image but it makes me uneasy. Although the boat's motor is turned off, the manatees are directly below the vessel. Manatees frequently hang out on the surface of the water and get cut by passing boat propellers. 1995.

38. Another clear day in the deepest spring at Three Sisters. 1995.

39. The water at the Big Spring is really clouded this day, but through the fog appears this big beautiful tarpon and two manatees off in the distance. 1995.

40. Cormorant and jacks. This spring looks like the setting for the Johnny Weissmuller Tarzan movies that I loved as I was growing up. The real setting for the Tarzan movies is about 50 miles away in the Silver River. I dove in that river recently. Along with the gators sunning on the banks are monkeys in the trees that are descendants of the original Tarzan monkeys. 1996. Split-toned.

41. A beautiful single tarpon glides past me at the Big Spring. 1995. Split-toned.

42. I call this picture *Mirrored Tarpon.* There are so many it's as if their images are reflected in a mirror. 1998.

43. I call this image *Smashmouth*, because it is likely that this fish was either caught and released or got away, but not without damage to its mouth. 1998.

44. More tarpon. 1998.

45. Tarpon with manatees who are warming themselves at the Big Spring. 1996.

46. Every year I see this school of mangrove snappers at the mouth to the Big Spring. 2001.

47. I call this picture *Starry Diver*, because the rain penetrating the water's surface looks like stars. 2001.

48. I call this photograph *Pisces*. 2001.

49. Fish under the mangroves. This is the natural environment, but close by the river has been greatly developed. 1999. Split-toned.

50. I was swimming at Three Sisters and the visibility underwater was really low. I raised my head to get my bearings and this magnificent great blue heron was in front of me. I saw this bird at this same site again in 2002. 2000.

51. A walk in the park, as if the manatee and diver
are out on a stroll. 1999.

Notes

Chapter 1. Those Were the Days . . .

1. For an excellent exhibit depicting aspects of the lives of the early Native residents of Florida, along with information regarding manatees, I suggest a visit to the South Florida Museum in Bradenton.

2. Peterson, "Man's Relationship with the Manatee," 22, citing C. B. Cory, *Hunting and Fishing in Florida, Including a Key to the Water Birds Known to Occur in the State* (Boston, Mass.: Estes and Lauriat, 1896).

3. Peterson, *ibid.*, 28, citing J. F. LeBaron, "The Manatee or Sea Cow," *Forest and Stream and Rod and Gun: The American Sportsman's Journal* 13 (1880): 1005–6. Ironically, LeBaron followed his verbiage about the plight of the manatee with an offer to guide sportsmen interested in hunting manatees.

4. Dr. Catherine Langtimm, who has conducted or helped conduct the adult survival estimates for the various subpopulations of manatees, has indicated that the estimated annual adult survival in the southwestern part of Florida is somewhat complicated by a less complete database for analysis than is the case elsewhere in the state. However, unpublished analyses presented by Langtimm and her colleagues at a workshop in April 2002 suggested that the estimated annual survival for adults in the more southern parts of southwestern Florida is variable among years but averages at only about 91 percent (with a range of about 87 to 94 percent). For the Atlantic coast, the most recent recalculations suggest that the mean annual survival rate is about 94 percent, but the rate appears to be declining in recent years.

Chapter 2. All in the Family

1. Daryl Domning commented when he edited this manuscript that this same logic might explain the disproportionate girth of Steller's sea cow.

2. O'Shea and Salisbury, "Belize—A Last Stronghold for Manatees," 156.

3. Stejneger, "How the Great Northern Sea Cow (*Rytina*) Became Exterminated," 1049.

Chapter 3. Vulnerable Giants

1. Captain Scammon was a well-known whaler, who has been immortalized by the fact that one of the gray whale calving grounds he discovered (and exploited) exists in what is now called Scammon's Lagoon. In 1874 Scammon published an interesting book entitled *The Marine Mammals of the Northwestern Coast of North America Together with an Account of the American Whale-Fishery.*

2. A useful definition of life history attributes is those traits (adaptations) for which variation directly affects fecundity, survival of individuals, and population growth. This definition is from Ricklefs, *Ecology*.

3. On the other hand, entanglement in fishing gear and ship strikes continue to kill right whales on a regular basis, so it is hard to argue that right whales are experiencing "the best of conditions."

Chapter 4. Searching for the Magic Number

1. See note 4 of chapter 1.

2. The calculated adult survival figures represent the percentage of the adults in a particular subpopulation that survive from one year to the next. The subpopulations that are in the best shape are those with high (mid-90%) and consistent values over time.

3. See note 4 of chapter 1.

4. Scientists consider a "manatee generation" to be about 15–17 years.

5. T. J. O'Shea, L. W. Lefebvre, and C. A. Beck, "Florida Manatees: Perspectives on Populations, Pain, and Protection," 31–43.

Chapter 5. "Misbehaving" Manatees in Harm's Way

1. Wartzok and Ketten, "Marine Mammal Sensory Systems," 155.

2. *Ibid.*, 160–61.

Chapter 6. Partnerships and Sharing

1. *Year of the Ocean Discussion Papers,* iii–v.

2. *Ibid.,* v.

3. Under the U.S. Endangered Species Act, "endangered" status applies to a species or population that is in imminent danger of extinction through all or part of its range. "Threatened" status applies to populations or species that could become endangered if appropriate protection is not provided.

4. Baur, Bean, and Gosliner, "The Laws Governing Marine Mammal Conservation in the United States," 70.

5. Reynolds, "Efforts to Conserve the Manatees," 287–89.

Chapter 7. Developing a Conservation Ethic

1. Mangel et al., "Principles for the Conservation of Wild Living Resources," 339.

2. Meffe, Perrin, and Dayton, "Marine Mammal Conservation," 437.

3. Domning, "Why Save the Manatee?" 167–73.

Further Reading

Ackerman, B. B., S. D. Wright, R. K. Bonde, C. A. Beck, and D. J. Banowetz. "Trends and Patterns in Mortality of Manatees in Florida." In *Population Biology of the Florida Manatee*, ed. T. J. O'Shea, B. B. Ackerman, and H. F. Percival, 223–58. Information and Technology Report 1. Washington, D.C.: National Biological Service, 1995.

Ames, A. L., and E. S. Van Vleet. "Organochlorine Residues in the Florida Manatee, *Trichechus manatus*." *Marine Pollution Bulletin* 32 (1996): 374–77.

Bangs, O. "The Present Standing of the Florida Manatee, *Trichechus manatus latirostris* (Harlan) in the Indian River Waters." *American Naturalist* 29 (1895): 783–87.

Baur, D. C., M. J. Bean, and M. L. Gosliner. "The Laws Governing Marine Mammal Conservation in the United States." In *Conservation and Management of Marine Mammals*, ed. J. R. Twiss and R. R. Reeves, 48–86. Washington, D.C.: Smithsonian Institution Press, 1999.

Beck, C. A., and J. P. Reid. "An Automated Photo-identification Catalog for Studies of the Life History of the Florida Manatee." In *Population Biology of the Florida Manatee*, ed. T. J. O'Shea, B. B. Ackerman, and H. F. Percival, 120–34. Information and Technology Report 1, Washington, D.C.: National Biological Service, 1995.

Boyd, I. L., C. Lockyer, and H. Marsh. "Reproduction in Marine Mammals." In *Biology of Marine Mammals*, ed. J. E. Reynolds III and S. A. Rommel, 218–86. Washington, D.C.: Smithsonian Institution Press, 1999.

Bullock, T. H., T. J. O'Shea, and M. C. McClune. "Auditory Evoked Potentials in the West Indian Manatee (Sirenia: *Trichechus manatus*)." *Journal of Comparative Physiology* 148: 547–54.

Burgess, J. C. "Biodiversity Loss through Tropical Deforestation: The Role of Timber Production and Trade." In *Biodiversity Conservation*, ed. C. A. Perrings, K. G. Maler, C. Folke, C. S. Holling, and B. O. Jansson, 237–55. Dordrecht, The Netherlands: Kluwar Academic Publishers, 1995.

Cohen, J. L., G. S. Tucker, and D. K. Odell. "The Photoreceptors of the West Indian Manatee." *Journal of Morphology* 173 (1982): 197–202.

Craig, B. A., M. A. Newton, R. A. Garrott, J. E. Reynolds III, and J. R. Wilcox. "Analysis of Aerial Survey Data on *Trichechus manatus* Using Markov Chain Monte Carlo." *Biometrics* 53 (1997): 524–41.

Dayton, P. K., M. J. Tegner, P. B. Edwards, and K. L. Riser. "Sliding Baselines, Ghosts, and Reduced Expectations in Kelp Forest Communities." *Ecological Applications* 8, no. 2 (1998): 309–22.

De Jong, W., A. Zweers, and M. Goodman. "Relationship of Aardvarks to Elephants, Hyraxes, and Sea Cows from Alpha-crystallin Sequences." *Nature* 292, no. 5823 (1981): 538–40.

Dimock, A. W. *Florida Enchantments*. New York: Frederick A. Stokes Company, 1926.

Domning, D. P. "Sea Cows and Sea Grasses." *Paleobiology* 7, no. 4 (1981): 417–20.

Domning, D. P. "Commercial Exploitation of Manatees *Trichechus* in Brazil c. 1785–1973." *Biological Conservation* 22 (1982): 101–26.

Domning, D. P. "Why Save the Manatee?" In *Manatees and Dugongs*, ed. J. E. Reynolds III and D. K. Odell, 167–73. New York: Facts on File, 1991.

Domning, D. P. "Evolution of the Sirenia and Desmostylia." In *Secondary Adaptations of Tetrapods to Life in Water*, ed. J. M. Mazin and V. de Buffrénil, 151–68. Munich, Germany: Verlag Dr. Friedrich Pfeil, 2001.

Domning, D. P. "Sirenians, Seagrasses, and Cenozoic Ecological Change in the Caribbean." *Palaeogeography, Palaeoclimatology, Palaeoecology* 166 (2001): 27–50.

Domning, D. P., and L. C. Hayek. "Interspecific and Intraspecific Morphological Variation in Manatees (Sirenia: *Trichechus*)." *Marine Mammal Science* 2, no. 2 (1986): 87–144.

Evans, P.G.H., and J. A. Raga. *Marine Mammals: Biology and Conservation*. New York: Kluwar Academic/Plenum Publishers, 2001.

Garrott, R. A., B. B. Ackerman, J. R. Cary, D. M. Heisey, J. E. Reynolds III, and J. R. Wilcox. "Trends in Counts of Florida Manatees at Winter Aggregation Sites." *Journal of Wildlife Management* 58 (1994): 642–54.

Gerstein, E. R., L. Gerstein, S. E. Forsythe, and J. E. Blue. "The Underwater Audiogram of the West Indian Manatee (*Trichechus manatus*)." *Journal of the Acoustical Society of America* 105, no. 6 (1999): 3575–83.

Griebel, U., and A. Schmid. "Color Vision in the Manatee (*Trichechus manatus*)." *Vision Research* 36 (1996): 2747–57.

Hartman, D. S. *Ecology and Behavior of the Manatee* (Trichechus manatus) *in Florida*. Special Publication no. 5. Lawrence, Kans.: American Society of Mammalogists, 1979.

Irvine, A. B. "Manatee Metabolism and Its Influence on Distribution in Florida." *Biological Conservation* 25 (1983): 315–34.

Ketten, D. R., D. K. Odell, and D. P. Domning. "Structure, Function, and Adaptation of the Manatee Ear." In *Marine Mammal Sensory Systems*, ed. J. Thomas, 77–95. New York: Plenum, 1992.

Langtimm, C. A., T. J. O'Shea, R. Pradel, and C. A. Beck. "Estimates of Annual Survival Probabilities for Adult Florida Manatees (*Trichechus manatus latirostris*)." *Ecology* 79 (1998): 981–97.

Lefebvre, L. W., M. Marmontel, J. P. Reid, G. B. Rathbun, and D. P. Domning. "Status and Biogeography of the West Indian Manatee." In *Biogeography of the West Indies*, ed. C. A. Woods and F. E. Sergile, 425–74. Boca Raton, Fla.: CRC Press, 2001.

Mangel, M., et al. "Principles for the Conservation of Wild Living Resources." *Ecological Applications* 6 (1996): 337–62.

Marine Mammal Commission. *Annual Report to Congress*. Bethesda, Md.: U.S. Marine Mammal Commission, 2001.

Marmontel, M., S. R. Humphrey, and T. J. O'Shea. "Population Viability Analysis of the Florida Manatee (*Trichechus manatus latirostris*), 1976–1991." *Conservation Biology* 11 (1997): 467–48.

Marsh, H., C. Eros, H. Penrose, and J. Hughes. *The Dugong* (Dugong dugon): *Status Reports and Action Plans for Countries and Territories in Its Range*. Townsville, Australia: Prepared for the World Conservation Union, the United Nations Environment Programme, the World Conservation Monitoring Centre, and the CRC Reef Research Centre, 2001.

Marshall, C. D., L. A. Clark, and R. L. Reep. "The Muscular Hydrostat of the Florida Manatee (*Trichechus manatus latirostris*): A Functional Morphological Model of Perioral Bristle Use." *Marine Mammal Science* 14 (1998): 290–303.

Meffe, G. K., W. F. Perrin, and P. K. Dayton. "Marine Mammal Conservation: Guiding Principles and Their Implementation." In *Conservation and Management of Marine Mammals*, ed. J. R. Twiss and R. R. Reeves, 437–54. Washington, D.C.: Smithsonian Institution Press, 1999.

Morales-Vela, B., D. Olivera-Gomez, J. E. Reynolds III, and G. B. Rathbun. "Distribution and Habitat Use by Manatees, *Trichechus manatus manatus*, in Belize and Chetumal Bay, Mexico." *Biological Conservation* 95 (2000): 67–75.

Oppel, F., and T. Meisel, eds. *Tales of Old Florida*. Secaucus, N.J.: Book Sales, 1987.

Ortiz, R. M., G.A.J. Worthy, and D. S. McKenzie. "Osmoregulation in Wild and Captive West Indian Manatees (*Trichechus manatus*)." *Physiological Zoology* 71 (1998): 449–57.

O'Shea, T. J. "Environmental Contaminants and Marine Mammals." In *Biology of Marine Mammals*, ed. J. E. Reynolds III and S. A. Rommel, 485–564. Washington, D.C.: Smithsonian Institution Press, 1999.

O'Shea, T. J., and R. L. Reep. "Encephalization Quotients and Life-history Traits in the Sirenia." *Journal of Mammalogy* 71 (1990): 534–43.

O'Shea, T. J., and C. A. Salisbury. "Belize—A Last Stronghold for Manatees in the Caribbean." *Oryx* 25 (1991): 156–64.

O'Shea, T. J., B. B. Ackerman, and H. F. Percival, eds. *Population Biology of the Florida Manatee*. Information and Technology Report 1. Washington, D.C.: National Biological Service, 1995.

O'Shea, T. J., C. A. Beck, R. K. Bonde, H. I. Kochman, and D. K. Odell. "An Analysis of Manatee Mortality Patterns in Florida, 1976–1981." *Journal of Wildlife Management* 49 (1985): 1–11.

O'Shea, T. J., L. W. Lefebvre, and C. A. Beck. "Florida Manatees: Perspectives on Populations, Pain, and Protection." In *The CRC Handbook of Marine Mammal Medicine*, 2d ed., ed. L. A. Dierauf and F.M.D. Gulland, 31–43. Boca Raton, Fla.: CRC Press, 2001.

O'Shea, T. J., J. F. Moore, and H. I. Kochman. "Contaminant Concentrations in Manatees (*Trichechus manatus*) in Florida." *Journal of Wildlife Management* 48 (1984): 741–48.

Pabst, D. A., S. A. Rommel, and W. A. McLellan. "The Functional Morphology of Marine Mammals." In *Biology of Marine Mammals*, ed. J. E. Reynolds III and S. A. Rommel, 15–72. Washington, D.C.: Smithsonian Institution Press, 1999.

Peterson, S. L. "Man's Relationship with the Florida Manatee, *Trichechus manatus latirostris* (Harlan): An Historical Perspective." M.A. thesis, University of Michigan, 1974.

Rathbun, G. B., and R. L. Wallace. "Florida Manatee." In *Endangered Animals: A Reference Guide to Conflicting Issues*, ed. R. P. Reading and B. Miller, 107–11. Westport, Conn.: Greenwood Press, 2000.

Rathbun, G. B., J. P. Reid, R. K. Bonde, and J. A. Powell. "Reproduction in Free-ranging Florida Manatees." In *Population Biology of the Florida Manatee*, ed. T. J. O'Shea, B. B. Ackerman, and H. F. Percival, 135–57. Information and Technology Report 1. Washington, D.C.: National Biological Service, 1995.

Reep, R. L., C. D. Marshall, M. L. Stoll, and D. M. Whitaker. "Distribution and Innervation of Facial Bristles and Hairs in the Florida Manatee (*Trichechus manatus latirostris*)." *Marine Mammal Science* 14 (1998): 257–73.

Reeves, R. R., B. S. Stewart, and S. Leatherwood. *The Sierra Club Handbook of Seals and Sirenians*. San Francisco, Calif.: Sierra Club Books, 1992.

Reynolds, J. E., III. "Herd Structure and Social Behavior of a Semi-isolated Colony of West Indian Manatees, *Trichechus manatus*." *Mammalia* 45 (1981): 431–51.

Reynolds, J. E. III. "Efforts to Conserve the Manatees." In *Conservation and Management of Marine Mammals*, ed. J. R. Twiss Jr. and R. R. Reeves, 267–95. Washington, D.C.: Smithsonian Institution Press, 1999.

Reynolds, J. E., III, and D. K. Odell. *Manatees and Dugongs*. New York: Facts on File, 1991.

Reynolds, J. E., III, and J. A. Powell. "Manatees (Trichechidae) (*Trichechus manatus, T. senegalensis*, and *T. inunguis*)." In *Encyclopedia of Marine Mammals*, ed. W. F. Perrin, B. Würsig, and J.G.M. Thewissen, 709–20. San Diego, Calif.: Academic Press, 2001.

Reynolds, J. E., III, and S. A. Rommel. "Structure and Function of the Gastrointestinal Tract of the Florida Manatee, *Trichechus manatus*." *The Anatomical Record* 245 (1996): 539–46.

Reynolds, J. E., III, D. P. DeMaster, and G. T. Silber. "Endangered and Threatened Species." In *Encyclopedia of Marine Mammals*, ed. W. F. Perrin, B. Würsig, and J.G.M. Thewissen, 373–82. San Diego, Calif.: Academic Press, 2001.

Reynolds, J. E., III, S. A. Rommel, and D. K. Odell. "Marine Mammals of the World." In *Biology of Marine Mammals*, ed. J. E. Reynolds III and S. A. Rommel. Washington, D.C.: Smithsonian Institution Press, 1999.

Reynolds, J. E., III, R. S. Wells, and S. D. Eide. *The Bottlenose Dolphin: Biology and Conservation*. Gainesville: University Press of Florida, 2000.

Ricklefs, R. E. *Ecology*. 3d ed. New York: W. H. Freeman and Co., 1990.

Ripple, J. *Manatees and Dugongs of the World*. Stillwater, Minn.: Voyageur Press, 1999.

Rommel, S. A., and J. E. Reynolds III. "Diaphragm Structure and Function in the Florida Manatee (*Trichechus manatus latirostris*)." *The Anatomical Record* 259 (2000): 41–51.

Rommel, S. A., D. A. Pabst, and W. A. McLellan. "Reproductive Thermoregulation in Marine Mammals." *American Naturalist* 86 (1995): 440–48.

Scammon, C. W. *The Marine Mammals of the Northwestern Coast of North America Together with an Account of the American Whale-Fishery*. New York: Dover Publications, 1968.

Stejneger, L. "How the Great Northern Sea Cow (*Rytina*) Became Exterminated." *American Naturalist* 21, no. 12 (1887): 1047–54.

Twiss, J. R., and R. R. Reeves, eds. *Conservation and Management of Marine Mammals*. Washington, D.C.: Smithsonian Institution Press, 1999.

U.S. Fish and Wildlife Service. *Florida Manatee Recovery Plan (Trichechus manatus latirostris)*. 3d rev. Atlanta, Ga.: Southeast Region, U.S. Fish and Wildlife Service, 2001.

Wallace, R. L. "The Florida Manatee Recovery Program: Unmasking Professional and Organizational Weaknesses." In *Endangered Species Recovery: Finding the Lessons, Improving the Process*, ed. T. W. Clark et al., 131–56. Washington, D.C.: Island Press, 1994.

Wallace, R. L. "A Review and Appraisal of the Florida Manatee Recovery Program." Available from R. Wallace, Eckerd College, St. Petersburg, Fla., 1999.

Wartzok, D., and D. R. Ketten. "Marine Mammal Sensory Systems." In *Biology of Marine Mammals*, ed. J. E. Reynolds III and S. A. Rommel, 117–75. Washington, D.C.: Smithsonian Institution Press, 1999.

Wells, R. S., D. J. Boness, and G. B. Rathbun. "Behavior." In *Biology of Marine Mammals*, ed. J. E. Reynolds III and S. A. Rommel, 324–422. Washington, D.C.: Smithsonian Institution Press, 1999.

Wilson, E. O. "Biological Diversity as a Scientific and Ethical Issue." In *Papers Read at the Joint Meeting of the Royal Society and the American Philosophical Society*. Vol. 1, 29–48. Philadelphia, Pa.: American Philosophical Society, 1987.

Worthy, G. A. J., and J. P. Hickie. "Relative Brain Size in Marine Mammals." *American Naturalist* 128 (1986): 445–59.

Year of the Ocean Discussion Papers. Washington, D.C.: Office of the Chief Scientist, National Oceanic and Atmospheric Administration, 1998.

Karen Glaser was born and raised in Pittsburgh, Pennsylvania. She has taught photography at Columbia College, Chicago, since 1980. Her photographs are in the permanent print collections of the Art Institute of Chicago, Museum of Fine Arts in Houston, Museum of Contemporary Photography in Chicago, Harry Ransom Center at the University of Texas in Austin, LaSalle Bank in Chicago, and David C. and Sarajean Ruttenberg Collection in Chicago, among others, as well as the digital archive of the Smithsonian Institution's National Museum of American Art. She has received a Ford Foundation Fellowship, a National Endowment for the Arts Visual Arts Regional Fellowship, and a Chairman's Grant from the Illinois Arts Council, and she has exhibited her photographs at more than 30 museums, universities, and galleries, including the Smithsonian Institution's National Museum of Natural History in Washington, D.C., Centro Colombo Americano in Medellín, Colombia, the Southeast Museum of Photography in Daytona Beach, Florida, Aperture's Burden Gallery in New York, the Museum of Contemporary Photography in Chicago, and the Museum of Fine Arts in Houston, among others. Ms. Glaser resides in Chicago, Illinois.

John E. Reynolds III serves as chairman of the United States Marine Mammal Commission, a position to which he was originally appointed in 1991 by President George Bush. He also serves as manatee research program manager at Mote Marine Laboratory in Sarasota, Florida, and as professor of marine science and biology at Eckerd College in St. Petersburg, Florida. In addition, he is the co-chair of the Sirenian Specialist Group for the International Union for the Conservation of Nature and Natural Resources. His 150-plus publications dealing with marine mammal biology and conservation include another book on manatees (*Manatees and Dugongs,* coauthored with Daniel K. Odell), a marine mammalogy text (*Biology of Marine Mammals,* coedited with Sentiel A. Rommel), and a recent University Press of Florida book titled *The Bottlenose Dolphin: Biology and Conservation* (coauthored with Randall S. Wells and Samantha D. Eide).